101
Meatless Family Dishes

Delicious and Satisfying Recipes
the Whole Family Will Love
(Even the Kids!)

John Ettinger

PRIMA PUBLISHING

PRIMA PUBLISHING and its colophon, which consists of the letter P over PRIMA, are trademarks of Prima Communications, Inc.

Cover photography © Kent Lacin Media Services, Sacramento

Library of Congress Cataloging-in-Publication Data

Ettinger, John.
    101 meatless family dishes: delicious and satisfying recipes the whole family will love (even the kids!)/John Ettinger.
        p.   cm.
    Includes index.
    ISBN 0-7615-0019-7 (pbk.)
        1. Vegetarian cookery.   2. Entrées (Cookery)   I. Title.
    II. Title: One hundred one meatless family dishes.   III. Title: One hundred and one meatless family dishes.
    TX837.E878   1995
    641.5'636—dc20

                                                                        95-3365
                                                                        CIP

99 00 01 AA 10 9 8 7 6 5 4 3 2
Printed in the United States of America

Nutritional Analyses:
A per serving nutritional breakdown is provided for each recipe. If a range is given for an ingredient amount, the breakdown is based on the smaller number. If a range is given for servings, the breakdown is based on the larger number. If a choice of ingredients is given in an ingredient listing, the breakdown is calculated using the first choice. Nutritional content may vary depending on the specific brands or types of ingredients used. "Optional" ingredients or those for which no specific amount is stated are not included in the breakdown. Nutritional figures are rounded to the nearest whole number.

How to Order:
Single copies may be ordered from Prima Publishing, P.O. Box 1260, Rocklin, CA 95677; telephone (916) 632-4400. Quantity discounts are also available. On your letterhead, include information concerning the intended use of the books and the number of books you wish to purchase.

Contents

Introduction

I confess that, as a child, not only did I eat my vegetables, I liked them. I grew up in California and I would like to say it was the availability of so many fresh fruits and vegetables that inspired my affection for the spinach and succotash rejected by many children. But in truth we ate a lot of frozen vegetables. My mother cooked for a small army each night (there were ten of us), and she just didn't shop daily for fresh vegetables. I do remember occasionally shelling fresh peas (and how delicious they were to eat fresh as we shelled), and frequent Brussels sprouts. I still love sprouts, as does one of my two sons (I believe they made a pact at birth, that each would loathe what the other loved in order to make meal preparation as difficult as possible).

Of course, for most Americans the idea of vegetables being "good for us" is something that didn't interest many of us until one or two or three dozen years later. Good health, always on the top of everyone's list, isn't as much about exercise anymore as it is about healthful cooking. Many who want a healthier life see that path lined with vegetables — and less red meat.

We want more healthful food but still yearn for meals that look and feel substantial, meals that remind us of those dinners we grew up with. This might be called a craving for old-fashioned vegetarian comfort food, replacing meat loaf with minestrone or pot roast with potpies — packed with veggies, of course. I hope you will enjoy substantial, more healthful meals time and again as a result of these recipes. For those unaccustomed to cooking vegetarian, I've included a guide to selecting and cooking the most popular fruits and vegetables, along with pound to cup equivalents and storage tips — always handy to have in one place.

Asparagus

Pick firm, straight spears with closed, compact tips or buds. Open heads are a sign of age and the asparagus may taste woody. Choose thick or thin spears; however, you may want to peel thick asparagus using a potato peeler. Select asparagus that is all the same size.

- Yield: One pound of asparagus equals 12 to 15 spears, 2 to $2^{1}/_{2}$ cups of cut pieces.
- Storage: Use asparagus as soon as possible. It will keep up to a week in the refrigerator, uncovered in the crisper.
- Preparation: Steam 7 to 10 minutes; stir-fry pieces in hot wok or skillet, with a little oil and 3 to 4 tablespoons water, 3 to 5 minutes; blanch in boiling water 3 to 5 minutes, then plunge into cold water; or microwave on high with $^{1}/_{4}$ cup water, covered, about 8 minutes, rearranging once halfway through cooking.

Broccoli

Choose a firm head with tightly closed buds. Avoid broccoli with yellow flowers, or loosely packed buds which may indicate an old head.

- Yield: One pound of broccoli yields about 4 to 5 cups of pieces.
- Storage: Broccoli will keep refrigerated for 2 or 3 days, stored in a plastic bag open on the bottom, with the stem wrapped in a wet cloth or paper towel.
- Preparation: Steam 7 to 10 minutes; stir-fry pieces in hot wok or skillet with a little oil and 5 to 6 tablespoons of water, 4 minutes; simmer in water, uncovered, 3 to 5 minutes, then plunge into cold water; or microwave on high in a covered, vented dish with $1/4$ cup water, 12 minutes, rotating dish twice during cooking.

Brussels Sprouts

Good Brussels sprouts should feel heavy for their size and have firm, tight heads. Pass up those with yellow or brown spots, or with loose outer leaves, and choose those that are small, green, and firm. Cut stems and take off outer leaves before cooking. Be careful to buy young, fresh sprouts and use them as soon as possible. Old ones have a sour and bitter taste.

- Yield: One-half pound of Brussels sprouts is about a dozen sprouts and yields 2 cups, trimmed.
- Storage: Don't store in an airtight bag; use an open or loose bag and keep in the refrigerator for up to 6 days.
- Preparation: Steam 10 to 15 minutes; simmer in water 10 to 14 minutes, uncovered, then plunge into cold water; or microwave on high in a covered dish with $1/4$ cup water, 5 to 6 minutes.

Cabbage

Red cabbage should not have any black edges while the best green cabbage has no brown streaks. Pick compact cabbages heavy for their size. Discard outer leaves before cooking.

- Yield: One trimmed 2-pound cabbage yields 9 to 10 cups sliced cabbage.
- Storage: Don't shred until ready to use. Store refrigerated in a tight plastic bag up to a week.
- Preparation: Steam, quartered, 10 to 12 minutes; stir-fry shredded in a little oil and 2 to 3 tablespoons water, 4 to 5 minutes; blanch halved or whole in boiling water, 6 to 8 minutes, then plunge into cold water; or microwave shredded 10 minutes, uncovered, on high, stirring once during cooking.

Carrots

The brighter the color the fresher the carrot. Good color and a firm texture are the keys.

- Yield: Two carrots yield 1 cup sliced or shredded carrots. One pound of carrots equals 4 cups sliced or shredded.
- Storage: Store in loose (not sealed) plastic bags in the refrigerator for several weeks.
- Preparation (sliced): Steam 5 to 8 minutes; stir-fry in oil 5 to 6 minutes; simmer in water 8 to 9 minutes, then plunge into cold water; or microwave with $^1/_4$ cup water, 10 to 14 minutes on high, covered, stirring once during cooking.

Cauliflower

Pick compact white heads that are surrounded by green leaves. Cauliflower should be firm and devoid of brown spots, and it should not have a strong smell.

- Yield: One pound, trimmed, yields 4 to 5 cups.
- Storage: Store refrigerated in loose plastic bag up to 8 days.
- Preparation: Steam, quartered or pieces, 6 to 9 minutes; stir-fry pieces in a little oil and 3 to 4 tablespoons water, 5 to 6 minutes; blanch quartered in boiling water 6 to 10

minutes, then plunge in cold water; or microwave pieces with $1/2$ cup water in covered dish, 10 to 12 minutes on high, stirring once during cooking.

Corn

When you press a fingernail into a fresh corn kernel it should spurt milk. Corn, more than most vegetables, is best when absolutely fresh. In Oregon we go to "U-pick" farms for fresh corn, since the minute corn is picked it begins to deteriorate. As quickly as 24 hours after picking the stem may become opaque or brown. Choose corn with a pointed end that is free from decay.

- Yield: Two ears will yield about 1 cup of kernels.
- Storage: Store in the refrigerator as is or, if husks have been removed, refrigerate in loose plastic bags for no more than 4 days.
- Preparation: Steam 5 to 7 minutes; or microwave husked corn on high with $1/4$ cup water, covered, 2 to 3 minutes per ear, rearranging halfway.

Eggplant

Choose eggplants with shiny skin which are heavy for their size. Fresh eggplant has a bright green cap. Avoid those with soft spots.

- Yield: One pound of eggplant, peeled and chopped, yields 2 cups.
- Storage: Keep eggplant wrapped in plastic in the refrigerator up to 3 days.
- Preparation: Steam quartered eggplant 10 to 12 minutes; blanch sliced or cubed eggplant 2 minutes, plunge in cold water; or microwave cubed pieces with 2 tablespoons water, covered, 5 to 6 minutes, stirring once during cooking.

Green Beans

If you can bend a green bean, don't buy it. Fresh beans should snap when bent and have no bulges. I look for thin beans with good color and wrinkle-free or even fuzzy pods.

- Yield: One pound of green beans yields 4 cups of cut beans.
- Storage: Refrigerate in loose bags up to 5 days.
- Preparation: Steam pieces 4 to 8 minutes; stir-fry in a little oil and 4 tablespoons water, covered, 5 to 6 minutes; blanch 2 to 3 minutes, then plunge into cold water; or microwave with $1/2$ cup of water, covered, 15 to 17 minutes, stirring after 7 to 8 minutes.

Leeks

Leeks have a milder taste than onions, and they may be substituted for onions in many recipes. Choose leeks that are firm and slender, less than 2 inches in diameter. Larger leeks are better suited for soups.

- Yield: One leek will yield 1 to $1^1/2$ cups chopped (white part only).
- Storage: Store in loose plastic bag in the crisper, with a wet paper towel, for up to 6 days.
- Preparation: Steam whole 7 to 8 minutes or add slices to a stir-fry for 4 to 5 minutes.

Lemons & Limes

To get more juice from a lemon or lime roll the fruit back and forth on a countertop several times, pressing it with your palm. If you need just a little juice, prick a few holes in the end and squeeze out drops. If you cook with the zest (grated skin) of these fruits, look for a zester in a specialty store; they work quite a bit better than a grater. Choose fruit without mold or soft spots. Look for a deep yellow or green color; avoid limes with brown spots.

- Yield: One lemon yields $1/4$ of juice. One lime yields $1/8$ to $1/4$ cup of juice.
- Storage: Store at room temperature or, if necessary, in the crisper of your refrigerator (but you get more juice from a fruit that isn't cold). Don't use plastic bags.

Mangoes & Papayas

Choose mangoes by smell; they are fragrant when ripe and often yellow in color. Green mangoes are not ripe and may have been picked too early. Fresh papayas give way to pressure, and are unwrinkled. Avoid bruised or soft mangoes or papayas.

- Yield: One mango yields about 1 cup of sliced fruit. One pound of papaya yields about $3/4$ cup of fruit.
- Storage: Store at room temperature until soft, then in a refrigerator up to 5 days. Do not cut until ready to serve.
- Preparation: Mango and papaya can be added to stir-fries. Stir in cut pieces just long enough to heat.

Peas

Snow peas, snap peas, and other peas should have a good green color. The pods should snap when bent. For best flavor, undercook your peas.

- Yield: One pound of snap peas yields 5 cups of peas. One pound of garden peas (unshelled) equals 1 cup of peas.
- Storage: Refrigerate unshelled in a plastic bag up to 6 days.
- Preparation: Steam shelled peas 3 to 4 minutes, snow peas 4 to 5 minutes; stir-fry snow peas 4 to 5 minutes in a little oil and 2 tablespoons water; blanch shelled peas in boiling water 2 minutes, snow peas $1^1/2$ minutes, then plunge in cold water; or microwave shelled peas on high with $1/4$ cup water, covered, 6 to 10 minutes.

Peppers

Sweet and hot peppers should have healthy stems and bright color in their skin. Usually the first signs of age in a pepper are soft spots near the cap or around the stem.

- Yield: One pound of medium peppers yields about $3^1/_2$ cups sliced peppers.
- Storage: Refrigerate, unbagged, in a crisper, 4 to 10 days, depending on the pepper — the sweeter the pepper (red, yellow) the more it will need refrigeration. Hot peppers may be stored at room temperature.
- Preparation: Steam sweet peppers 4 to 5 minutes or stir-fry in a little oil and 3 tablespoons of water 4 to 5 minutes.

Pineapples

The inner leaves of a ripe pineapple will come out easily. The fruit should be heavy for its size.

- Yield: A 3-pound pineapple yields 3 cups of fruit.
- Storage: Store at room temperature until slightly soft, then refrigerate.
- Preparation: Pineapple can be added to stir-fries. Stir in cut pieces just long enough to heat.

Spinach, Chicory, Romaine

Spinach should have dark green, crisp leaves and a strong earthy smell. Avoid chicory that looks yellow or limp, and remember that large leaves may be bitter. The best romaine is crisp, with a deep green color.

- Yield: One bunch of greens equals about $^3/_4$ pound. One pound of fresh spinach yields about 1 cup cooked.
- Storage: Store spinach in the refrigerator, wrapped in a towel. Store chicory in a loose plastic bag in the refrigerator. Refrigerate romaine in a closed bag. All will last up to a week.

- Preparation: Steam spinach 4 to 5 minutes, until wilted; stir-fry spinach in a little oil 4 to 5 minutes; or microwave 5 to 7 minutes, covered, stirring once during cooking.

Sweet Potatoes

Pick firm potatoes with no soft spots or bruises.

- Yield: One pound of sweet potatoes(3 potatoes) yields about 5 cups of cubed potatoes.
- Storage: Store in a dark, cool place, but don't refrigerate.
- Preparation: Steam sweet potato pieces 12 to 15 minutes, steam whole potatoes 30 to 40 minutes; stir-fry in a little oil and 4 tablespoons water 10 to 12 minutes; or microwave cubed potatoes on high with 1/2 cup water, covered, 9 minutes, stirring once during cooking; prick and bake whole 40 minutes at 400°.

Tomatoes

During the winter, use canned tomatoes rather than fresh ones, unless you have vine-ripened hothouse tomatoes available. In season, choose firm tomatoes with bright color.

- Yield: Three tomatoes yield 3 to 4 cups chopped.
- Storage: Store at room temperature 3 to 4 days.
- Preparation: Add chopped tomatoes to stir-fries just long enough to heat. (See page 14 for information on roasting and seeding tomatoes.)

Turnips

Small turnips are best, and turnips don't last long fresh so it's important to pick ones that still have their moisture. Choose firm vegetables with a smooth appearance. If the tops are still on, look for good green color.

- Yield: One pound trimmed turnips yields 4 cups chopped.

- Storage: Store turnips unbagged in the refrigerator up to 5 days.
- Preparation: Steam whole turnips 25 minutes; stir-fry in a little oil and 4 tablespoons water 6 to 12 minutes; boil 15 minutes, uncovered; or microwave on high, covered, with 3 tablespoons water 10 minutes, stirring once during cooking.

Zucchini

Buy smooth, firm, small, young zucchini with bright green skin.

- Yield: One pound yields about $3^{1}/2$ cups cubed.
- Storage: Refrigerate in a loose bag up to 1 week.
- Preparation: Steam sliced zucchini 10 minutes; stir-fry in a little oil and 2 tablespoons water 10 minutes; or microwave cubed or sliced zucchini on high, covered, with $^{1}/4$ cup water, 10 to 12 minutes, stirring once during cooking.

Three basic recipes are used in a number of these *101 Meatless Family Dishes.*

Pizza Dough

I frequently use the refrigerated dough found with the cookies and biscuits in the grocery store, especially for calzone. It's quick and easy, and works well. When I'm feeling ambitious, I use this dough recipe.

$^{2}/3$ cup warm water (110 to 115°)
1 package active dry yeast (about 2 teaspoons)
$^{1}/4$ teaspoon sugar
2 cups all-purpose flour
$^{1}/4$ teaspoon salt

Place the water, yeast, and sugar in a mixing bowl. Stir, then let rest for 5 minutes. Add the flour and salt and mix with a dough hook for 3 minutes or by hand for 5 minutes.

Place the dough in a large bowl, cover with plastic wrap, and set in a warm place for about 2 hours, or until the dough has doubled. Serves six.

Each Serving Provides:
155 calories, 5g protein, 0g fat, 32g carbohydrate,
0mg cholesterol, 1g dietary fiber, 135mg sodium

Pie or Tart Shells

There are some good prepared shells available; for home-made pies and tarts, use this recipe.

2^1/$_2$ tablespoons unsalted butter, cold
1 cup unbleached all-purpose flour
^{1}/$_8$ teaspoon salt
5 tablespoons ice water

Cut butter into 1-inch pieces. Combine flour, butter, and salt; mix until butter pieces are well coated with flour. Add 2^1/$_2$ tablespoons water and, using two knives, cut through mixture to mix in water and cut up the butter pieces. Add the remaining 2^1/$_2$ tablespoons water over the dry parts of the dough, then cut in until all of the flour is damp. Roll the dough into a ball and dust with flour. Wrap in plastic and refrigerate for 2 hours. Roll out the dough on a floured board into a 12-inch diameter. Place on a cookie sheet, cover, and chill at least 1 hour. Serves six.

Each Serving Provides:
123 calories, 2g protein, 5g fat, 16g carbohydrate,
14mg cholesterol, 1g dietary fiber, 46mg sodium

Vegetable Broth

Unfortunately, many canned vegetable broths leave something to be desired. You can use canned if necessary, but making your own is pretty easy. Here's my recipe for vegetable broth.

2 large onions, coarsely chopped
3 stalks celery, coarsely chopped
1 white turnip, peeled and coarsely chopped
1 whole garlic bulb, unpeeled, quartered
1 bunch parsley
10 carrots, coarsely chopped
3 cups chopped lettuce
2 teaspoons fresh minced thyme or $^1/2$ teaspoon dried
2 teaspoons fresh minced marjoram or $^1/2$ teaspoon dried
2 teaspoons pepper
4 quarts water

Place all vegetables and spices in a large pot and add water. Bring to a boil then lower heat and simmer, partially covered, until vegetables become soft (about an hour). Pour soup through a colander, pressing the vegetables to extract juices. Discard solids. Pour broth through cheesecloth or a strainer. Cool before refrigerating.

Each 1-Cup Serving Provides:
10 calories, 1g protein, 0g fat, 2g carbohydrate,
0mg cholesterol, 0g dietary fiber, 4mg sodium

Finally, here are a few notes on this book and some tips for healthful cooking.

- I prefer olive and canola oils. Extra-virgin olive oil is highly recommended for dressings and other recipes with uncooked olive oil.

- Use fresh, not dried, parsley. Washed and dried parsley chops easily and, like other herbs, lasts a couple of weeks in the refrigerator when the top is covered in plastic while the bottom is wrapped in a wet paper napkin. For most other herbs you can substitute dried, unless otherwise specified in the recipe.

- Choose Parmesan cheese to grate yourself or freshly grated cheese from the deli section. That way you'll skip the preservatives in the packaged types and enjoy a much better-tasting cheese.

- Use lowfat or nonfat ricotta, cottage cheese, yogurt, and sour cream in these recipes.

- Buy fresh ginger. Powdered ginger is a completely different spice. None of these recipes calls for powdered ginger and you should never substitute powdered in any recipe calling for fresh. The same is true, of course, for fresh cilantro and ground coriander. Coriander is the seed, cilantro is the leaf; they are not even the same spice.

- Don't be disappointed if jalapeños are the only fresh hot pepper you can find. Serranos and arbols are a little hotter so use a little more jalapeño if substituting.

- Always use **caution** when cooking with hot peppers. A little pepper on the finger, inadvertently rubbed into the eye a little later, is extremely painful and even dangerous. Use gloves and/or wash up well after using hot peppers.

- When you buy packaged curry or chili powder, be sure to purchase high-quality combinations. Some discount and store brands may have an off taste due to inferior ingredients. Good ingredients yield the best results; it's worth the effort to find good powders in a specialty cookware shop or catalog.

- Don't overcook vegetables. The key to great flavor is to slightly undercook them. Taste as you go if you are unsure of the time.

- **Beans** If you want to use dried black, red, or white beans rather than canned, soak them overnight in cold water, after first picking out any stones. To quick-soak beans: cover with water and bring to a boil. Boil, covered, for a couple of minutes, remove from heat, and let sit 1 to $1^{1}/_{2}$ hours. Drain and use fresh water for cooking. I use both canned and fresh, depending upon the time I have to make the dish.

- **Tomatoes** A few of the recipes call for peeled tomatoes. To peel and seed tomatoes, drop into boiling water for about 15 seconds. Drain and peel. Cut the tomatoes in half crosswise and gently squeeze out the seeds.

- **Peppers** To roast hot or sweet peppers, first char under a broiler, turning frequently, until blackened. Put in a paper bag, close tightly, and let steam for 20 minutes or so. The skin should come off quickly and easily. Jars of roasted peppers are also available in grocery stores and many of them are of pretty good quality. Again, if you have the time, roast your own; if not, open a jar.

I hope you enjoy my recipes.

Soups, Stews, & Chilis

I f you want to know the warming value of soup, come to Oregon, where the damp, frequently all too gloomy winter months can make you feel as though the hovering clouds have invaded your arteries.

It isn't that it rains a lot in western Oregon; where I live we get just 32 inches or so in a year. It's just that the sun doesn't appear very often. I recall one February where the sun shone only three or four days of the month.

During long stretches of low clouds filled with Canada mist (it missed Canada and came to Oregon), a warm, sturdy soup or stew is very welcome with fresh, hot bread or rolls.

Here are a few soups to take the winter chill out of your bones, plus a couple of cool summer soups.

Minestrone

Preparation time: 30 minutes (plus 2 hours cooking time)

Minestrone, the marriage of pasta, beans, and vegetables,
is a flexible soup. Substitute other vegetables for the ones
here if you like. I've replaced the pasta with arborio rice,
but you can use regular rice as well.

1 can (16 ounces) tomatoes with juice, or 2 fresh
   tomatoes
1 clove garlic, minced
2 tablespoons shredded fresh basil, or 1 tablespoon
   dried
2 tablespoons olive oil
1 tablespoon butter or another tablespoon of oil
2 onions, finely chopped
1 cup cooked cannellini beans (see page 13) or 1 cup
   canned, drained
2 carrots, diced
1 zucchini, diced
2 potatoes, peeled and diced
1 cup shredded cabbage
1 cup trimmed and cut green beans (1" pieces)
2 teaspoons dried thyme
1 teaspoon dried oregano
$1/4$ teaspoon pepper
$1/8$ teaspoon salt
4 quarts water
1 cup arborio rice
3 tablespoons minced parsley
Grated Parmesan cheese (optional)

Purée the tomatoes with garlic, basil, and olive oil and set aside. In a pot, heat butter and add onions. Cook until soft, about 6 minutes, then add cannellini beans, carrots, and zucchini and cook another 5 minutes. Add potatoes, cabbage, green beans, spices, tomato purée, and water. Bring to a boil, cover, and simmer until cannellini beans are soft, 60 to 90 minutes, stirring occasionally. Stir in the rice, cover and cook another 20 minutes, stirring frequently. (If you use long-grain rather than arborio rice, just stir in the rice, cover and cook.) Add parsley and serve topped with Parmesan if desired.

Serves 4

Each Serving Provides:
615 calories, 21g protein, 12g fat, 110g carbohydrate,
8mg cholesterol, 10g dietary fiber, 335mg sodium

Avocado Gazpacho

Preparation time: 25 minutes (plus 1 hour chilling time)

Avocado gives this version of gazpacho a creamy lift. If you use a food processor to chop the vegetables be careful not to overprocess. Serve chilled with warm tortillas and the remaining avocado slices.

2 sweet onions
1 cucumber, peeled and seeded
2 bell peppers, seeded
6 small ripe tomatoes, peeled (see page 14)
2 cloves garlic
1 jalapeño pepper, seeded
2 cups tomato juice
$^1/_2$ cup extra-virgin olive oil
$^1/_4$ teaspoon salt
$^1/_4$ teaspoon pepper
2 small avocados, peeled and seeded, with half of 1
    avocado cut into slices
Juice of $^1/_2$ lemon (about $1^1/_2$ tablespoons)
Sour cream (optional)

Finely chop onions, cucumber, bell peppers, and 4 tomatoes and place in a bowl. In a blender or food processor add the remaining ingredients, except the avocado, lemon juice, and sour cream, and purée; then combine the chopped vegetables with the purée. Purée the unsliced

1¹/₂ avocadoes with lemon juice, then stir into the center of the soup. Chill one hour. Serve with sour cream if desired, and garnish with a slice of avocado in each bowl.

Serves 4

Each Serving Provides:
504 calories, 6g protein, 43g fat, 32g carbohydrate,
0mg cholesterol, 7g dietary fiber, 601mg sodium

Asian Gazpacho

Preparation time: 40 minutes (plus 1 hour chilling time)

This is an Asian twist on the traditional Spanish cold soup. It makes a nice light meal by itself, or serve with a salad.

$^1/_2$ cucumber, peeled and chopped
$^1/_2$ zucchini, diced into small pieces
1 red pepper, seeded and finely chopped
$^1/_2$ cup finely chopped daikon (large Oriental radish)
$^1/_2$ cup finely chopped leeks
$^1/_2$ cup finely chopped shiitake or button mushrooms
$^1/_3$ cup chopped fresh cilantro
2 tablespoons tamari or soy sauce
$^1/_4$ teaspoon red pepper flakes
$^1/_2$ cup rice vinegar
2 teaspoons sesame oil
3 cups vegetable broth, chilled

Combine the cucumber, zucchini, red pepper, daikon, leeks, mushrooms, and cilantro and set aside. Mix together remaining ingredients, except the broth, in a bowl, then combine with vegetables. Add broth and mix well, then chill one hour before serving.

Serves 4

Each Serving Provides:
77 calories, 3g protein, 3g fat, 12g carbohydrate,
0mg cholesterol, 2g dietary fiber, 518mg sodium

Black Bean Stew

Preparation time: 35 minutes

I always keep black beans on hand; they're versatile for soups, tacos, even pastas and pasta salads. I make this dish stew-like, but you can make it soupy by using more liquid.

2 tablespoons vegetable oil
2 onions, chopped
1 bell pepper, seeded and diced
4 cloves garlic, minced or chopped
4 cups cooked black beans (see page 13)
   or 1 can (16 ounces), rinsed and drained
2 to 3 cups water or vegetable broth (more for a
   soup-like dish, less for stew)
1 tablespoon dried oregano
1 tablespoon chili powder
2 teaspoons cumin
$1/4$ teaspoon cayenne pepper
1 tomato, chopped
$1/2$ cup chopped fresh cilantro
$1/3$ cup wine vinegar

Heat oil and sauté onions and pepper for 5 minutes, until soft. Add garlic and sauté another 2 minutes. Meanwhile, combine beans and water in a separate pot and bring to a simmer. Add onion mixture to the beans, then add spices and simmer, covered, for 15 minutes. Add remaining ingredients and return to a boil. Simmer 5 minutes and serve.

Serves 4

Each Serving Provides:
801 calories, 45g protein, 11g fat, 139g carbohydrate, 0mg cholesterol, 29g dietary fiber, 44mg sodium

Spicy Corn & Black Bean Stew

Preparation time: 20 minutes (plus 2 hours cooking time)

Fresh cilantro offers a refreshing contrast to the spiciness of this soup. I serve it with sour cream.

1 tablespoon olive oil
1 small onion, chopped
4 cloves garlic, minced or chopped
1 carrot, thinly sliced
1 stalk celery, thinly sliced
2 jalapeños, seeded and minced
2 bell peppers, red or green, seeded and diced
7 cups vegetable broth or water
4 cups corn, fresh (cut from 8 ears) or frozen
1 can (16 ounces) black beans, rinsed and drained,
   or 2 cups cooked (see page 13)
3 teaspoons cumin
2 teaspoons ground coriander
1 teaspoon dried oregano
4 tablespoons minced fresh cilantro
Sour cream, yogurt, or salsa (optional)

Heat oil and sauté onion in oil 5 minutes, until soft. Add garlic for another minute, then add carrot, celery, and peppers, and continue to sauté 5 minutes over medium-low heat. Add remaining ingredients, except cilantro and optional ingredients; cover, and barely simmer over low heat 2 hours. Ladle into bowls and add a little cilantro on top. Serve with sour cream, yogurt, or salsa if desired.

Serves 4

Each Serving Provides:
347 calories, 15g protein, 6g fat, 68g carbohydrate, 0mg cholesterol, 7g dietary fiber, 502mg sodium

Southwestern Stew
with Jalapeño Paste

Preparation time: 50 minutes

This thick, stovetop stew uses jalapeño paste for an even spiciness. Use the extra paste for sandwiches or to stir into other soups.

2 jalapeños, seeded and coarsely chopped
6 tablespoons vegetable oil
1 teaspoon ground coriander
2 tablespoons olive or vegetable oil
1 onion, diced
4 cloves garlic, minced
2 bell peppers, green, yellow, or red, seeded and
   diced
2 zucchinis, diced
1 teaspoon ground cumin
1 teaspoon dried oregano
$1/4$ teaspoon salt
$1/4$ teaspoon pepper
1 can (28 ounces) tomatoes with juice, chopped
$1^1/2$ cups corn kernels, fresh (cut from 3 ears) or
   frozen
3 tablespoons chopped fresh cilantro
2 tablespoons chopped fresh parsley
Sour cream (optional)

Make a paste by placing the jalapeños in a bowl; cover with boiling water for 20 minutes. Drain and place in a blender with 6 tablespoons of vegetable oil and coriander and purée to a paste. Set aside.

Meanwhile, heat olive oil in a skillet and sauté onion, garlic, and peppers 10 minutes, until just soft. Add zucchini, cumin, oregano, salt, and pepper and sauté 5 more minutes. Add tomatoes, and half the jalapeño paste (or more to taste). Heat for a couple of minutes, then add the corn and bring to a boil. Simmer, covered, for 30 minutes, stirring occasionally. Stir in the cilantro and parsley and serve with sour cream if desired.

Serves 4

Each Serving Provides:
406 calories, 6g protein, 29g fat, 36g carbohydrate, 0mg cholesterol, 6g dietary fiber, 466mg sodium

Lemon Pasta e Fagioli

Preparation time: 25 minutes

Pasta e Fagioli remains the soup of the poor in many parts of the world. This version, adding hot pepper and a lemon finish, makes a filling dinner served with bread.

$^{1}/_{2}$ pound rigatoni or other pasta
3 tablespoons olive oil
$^{1}/_{2}$ onion, minced
4 cloves garlic, minced
1 jalapeño, seeded and minced
1 red bell pepper, seeded and diced
1 stalk celery, chopped
2 cups cooked cannellini beans (see page 13) or
    1 can (16 ounces), drained
1 can (28 ounces) tomatoes with juice, chopped
3 tablespoons lemon juice
2 tablespoons chopped parsley

Cook pasta according to package directions until half done, drain. Meanwhile, heat oil in a large pot and sauté onion, garlic, peppers, and celery over medium-low heat for 5 minutes. Add beans and tomatoes and cook gently for 5 minutes. Add lemon juice, parsley, and pasta and continue to cook until pasta is done. Let stand 5 minutes to let flavors blend before serving.

Serves 4

Each Serving Provides:
693 calories, 32g protein, 13g fat, 117g carbohydrate,
0mg cholesterol, 11g dietary fiber, 348mg sodium

Sweet Pepper Soup

Preparation time: 45 minutes.

I love sweet peppers raw, sautéed, barbecued, even puréed, as they are in this soup. To make this rich-colored soup quickly, I use the jars of roasted reds.

2 tablespoons olive oil
1 onion, coarsely chopped
2 red bell peppers, seeded and coarsely chopped
2 cloves garlic, peeled and halved
3 cups vegetable broth
2 roasted red peppers (see page 14) or 1 jar (7 ounces)
1 tablespoon good-quality chili powder
1 teaspoon paprika
$1/8$ teaspoon cayenne
$1/2$ cup whole almonds

Heat oil in a saucepan and add onion and bell peppers. Sauté, stirring, for 10 minutes. Add garlic and sauté another 5 minutes. Add broth, roasted peppers, chili powder, paprika, and cayenne and simmer, uncovered, for 20 minutes. Remove onion, peppers, and garlic from the pan and place in a blender. Add almonds and $1/2$ cup of liquid from the soup and blend until smooth. Return purée to pan, stir and simmer 5 minutes.

Serves 4

Each Serving Provides:
*207 calories, 5g protein, 15g fat, 16g carbohydrate,
0mg cholesterol, 4g dietary fiber, 983mg sodium*

Tomato & Lentil Soup

Preparation time: 20 minutes (plus 55 minutes cooking time)

This simple, healthful, and delicious soup is great fresh or as a leftover for lunch. Serve with a green or vegetable salad and crackers, if desired.

2 tablespoons olive oil
1 large onion, chopped
2 cloves garlic, minced
1 red bell pepper, seeded and chopped
1 cup lentils
2 1/2 cups vegetable broth
2 teaspoons dried thyme
1 teaspoon dried basil
2 tomatoes, diced, or 1 can (15 ounces) with juice
1 tablespoon lemon zest
2 tablespoons lemon juice

Heat oil in a pot and sauté the onion, garlic, and pepper until soft. Add lentils, broth, thyme, and basil and bring to a boil. Reduce heat and simmer, about 45 minutes, then add remaining ingredients and heat 10 minutes.

Serves 4

Each Serving Provides:
285 calories, 16g protein, 8g fat, 42g carbohydrate,
0mg cholesterol, 8g dietary fiber, 14mg sodium

Mexican Dry Soup

Preparation time: 20 minutes

This traditional soup is called a dry soup because the broth is absorbed, leaving a "dry" soup. It can be made with more broth, for those who want it "soupy."

12 ounces dried fedelini or vermicelli
3 tablespoons olive oil
$^1/_2$ red bell pepper, seeded and diced
1 onion, chopped
3 cloves garlic
2 tomatoes, peeled and chopped
1 tablespoon chile powder
3 cups vegetable broth or water
Grated Parmesan cheese (optional)

Leave the pasta in its bag and crush with a rolling pin. Heat 2 tablespoons of the oil in a skillet, add pasta and stir constantly until lightly browned, about 4 to 5 minutes. Meanwhile, in another pan, heat remaining 1 tablespoon oil and sauté pepper until soft, about 5 minutes.

Place onion, garlic, tomatoes, and chile powder in a blender and purée. Add purée to the pasta, then add broth or water and red pepper. Cover and cook over low heat 10 minutes, or until all of the moisture is absorbed. Spoon into bowls and top with cheese, if desired.

Serves 4

Each Serving Provides:
465 calories, 13g protein, 12g fat, 76g carbohydrate,
0mg cholesterol, 5g dietary fiber, 35mg sodium

Black & Red Bean Chili

Preparation time: 25 minutes (plus 1 hour and 15 minutes cooking time)

This chili is best with dried beans, but you can use canned if you want to make it the same day. Serve with tortillas or cornbread.

1 cup cooked black beans (see page 13) or 1 can (8 ounces) beans, drained and rinsed
1 cup cooked kidney beans (see page 13) or 1 can (8 ounces), drained
3 tablespoons vegetable oil
2 onions, chopped
1 teaspoon seeded and chopped serrano pepper (more to taste)
2 tablespoons seeded and chopped Anaheim pepper (or canned green chiles)
4 teaspoons ground cumin
4 teaspoons sweet paprika
3 teaspoons dried oregano
2 tablespoons good-quality chili powder
3 cloves garlic, minced or chopped
3 medium tomatoes, peeled, with juice or 1 can (28 ounces)
1/4 cup chopped cilantro
Salt and pepper
Grated cheddar or jack cheese (optional)
Warm tortillas

Place beans in a large pot and cover with water by about 2 inches. Bring to boil then reduce to simmer.

Heat oil in a skillet, sauté onions and peppers (if fresh — do not sauté canned green chiles) until soft, then add herbs, spices, garlic, and tomatoes with juice. Simmer about 15 minutes then add to the beans and cover with water by about an inch (if needed). Cook slowly for an hour, adding more water if necessary to keep beans covered. Add cilantro and cook another 15 minutes.

Taste and add salt and pepper as needed. Top with cheese if desired and serve with warm tortillas.

Serves 4

Each Serving Provides:
450 calories, 20g protein, 14g fat, 67g carbohydrate,
0mg cholesterol, 15g dietary fiber, 103mg sodium

Mexican Vegetable Soup

Preparation time: 30 minutes

The ancho pepper, oregano, and chili powder give this a delightful Mexican flavor. Serve with warm tortillas.

1 dried ancho chile, stemmed and seeded
$1/2$ teaspoon good-quality chili powder
2 tablespoons vegetable oil
1 onion, diced
2 cloves garlic, minced
1 zucchini, trimmed and cut into pieces
2 carrots, sliced
1 can (15 ounces) tomatoes, chopped
6 cups vegetable broth or water
1 cup canned garbanzo beans, drained
1 teaspoon dried oregano
3 tablespoons fresh lemon juice (about 1 lemon)
3 tablespoons minced cilantro

Place ancho chile in a bowl and pour hot water on top. Let soak 15 minutes, place in a blender with chili powder and a little of the water, and purée. Set aside.

Combine oil, onion, and garlic in a pot and heat, stirring until onions are soft, about 5 minutes. Add zucchini, carrots, tomatoes, and broth, bring to a boil, and simmer 10 minutes. Add garbanzo beans and oregano and simmer another 10 minutes. Combine lemon juice with pureed pepper mixture and add to the soup. Ladle into bowls and top with cilantro.

Serves 4

Each Serving Provides:
238 calories, 7g protein, 9g fat, 36g carbohydrate,
0mg cholesterol, 6g dietary fiber, 406mg sodium

Cream of Chick-Pea Soup

Preparation time: 20 minutes (plus 1 hour cooking time)

Don't over-purée this soup; it's better when left with a 9

little texture. It's great served with a green salad and a simple vinaigrette.

2 tablespoons oil
1 onion, chopped
4 cloves garlic, minced
1 carrot, chopped
$^1/_2$ yellow bell pepper, seeded and sliced
$^1/_4$ teaspoon red pepper flakes
$^1/_4$ teaspoon ground cumin
$^1/_2$ teaspoon dried oregano
7 cups vegetable broth
1 cup canned chick-peas (garbanzo beans)
1 cup yogurt
2 tablespoons minced parsley

Heat oil in a large pot and sauté onion until soft, about 5 minutes. Add garlic, carrot, pepper, red pepper flakes, cumin, and oregano and cook another 6 to 7 minutes. Add broth and chick-peas and bring to a boil. Cover and simmer for about an hour, stirring occasionally.

Using a slotted spoon, remove vegetables to a
blender. Add yogurt and purée (you will probably need to
add some of the cooking liquid to the purée). Return
purée to the remaining water in the pot and stir in parsley.

Serves 4

Each Serving Provides:
227 calories, 8g protein, 9g fat, 29g carbohydrate,
4mg cholesterol, 4g dietary fiber, 237mg sodium

Potato & Leek Soup
with Cilantro or Watercress

Preparation time: 45 minutes

A simple, filling, and warm treat on a cool night. This
soup is wonderful as is or, to spruce it up, you may add
cilantro, watercress, or even parsley.

3 tablespoons butter
4 cups (about 1 pound) leeks, trimmed, cleaned and
  chopped
2 stalks celery, sliced
3 cups water
2 potatoes, peeled and diced
3 cups milk
1/8 teaspoon salt
1/4 teaspoon pepper
1/2 cup chopped cilantro or watercress (optional)

Melt butter in a pot, add the leeks and celery, and cook
over low heat 15 minutes, stirring frequently. Add water,
potatoes, milk, salt, and pepper. Cover and cook 20 minutes, stirring frequently, or until potatoes are tender.
Remove to a blender or food processor and purée. Stir in
cilantro or watercress, or sprinkle on top and serve.

Serves 4

Each Serving Provides:
297 calories, 9g protein, 13g fat, 38g carbohydrate,
38mg cholesterol, 3g dietary fiber, 296mg sodium

Rice and Mushroom Soup

Preparation time: 45 minutes

This is a filling soup, great with bread or breadsticks. You may substitute another rice for the arborio. If you do, disregard the instruction to stir frequently.

2 tablespoons butter
2 tablespoons extra-virgin olive oil
1 onion, finely chopped
$^1/_2$ pound fresh mushrooms, sliced
$^1/_4$ cup chopped fresh basil or 1$^1/_2$ tablespoons dried
1 teaspoon dried sage
$^1/_2$ teaspoon pepper
1 can (15 ounces) tomatoes, with juice
3$^1/_2$ cups water
$^1/_2$ cup arborio rice
Grated Parmesan cheese (optional)

Melt the butter with oil in a pot. Stir in onion and sauté until soft, 6 to 7 minutes. Add mushrooms, basil, sage, and pepper and cook another 5 minutes, stirring frequently. Stir in tomatoes, cover, and cook 10 minutes.

Add water to pot and bring to a boil. Add rice, combine well, cover and simmer, stirring frequently, until the rice is done, about 20 minutes. Serve topped with cheese if desired.

Serves 4

Each Serving Provides:
270 calories, 4g protein, 14g fat, 34g carbohydrate,
17mg cholesterol, 3g dietary fiber, 266mg sodium

Chunky Cream of Tomato Soup with Rice & Mushrooms

Preparation time: 45 minutes

Don't over-process this soup; let some of the texture of the tomatoes come through. Add some red pepper flakes if you like it spicier.

3 tablespoons extra-virgin olive oil
$^1/_2$ bell pepper, seeded and chopped
3 cloves garlic, minced
1 onion, chopped
$5^1/_2$ cups vegetable broth
1 teaspoon dried dill
2 tablespoons chopped fresh basil
$^1/_2$ teaspoon dried thyme
2 pounds fresh plum tomatoes, peeled and seeded,
   or canned tomatoes, drained
$^1/_2$ cup tomato paste
1 tablespoon minced celery
5 mushrooms, sliced
$^1/_2$ cup rice
$^1/_4$ cup heavy cream

Heat 1 tablespoon of oil and add the pepper, 2 of the garlic cloves, and all but 2 tablespoons of onion. Sauté over low heat 10 minutes, until vegetables are soft. Heat $4^1/_2$ cups of broth in a pot and add vegetables, dill, basil, and thyme and stir. Add tomatoes and tomato paste, increase heat and stir, bringing to a simmer. Cover and simmer 25 minutes.

Meanwhile, heat remaining 2 tablespoons oil and sauté the remaining 2 tablespoons onion, 1 clove garlic, and celery for 5 minutes. Add mushrooms and cook another 4 minutes. Add rice and cook, stirring constantly, 1 to 2 minutes. Add remaining 1 cup broth and bring to a boil. Cover, reduce heat, and cook 18 minutes.

Remove tomato mixture to a blender and coarsely purée in batches, leaving some texture. Stir in cream, add the cooked rice mixture, and serve.

Serves 4

Each Serving Provides:
355 calories, 7g protein, 17g fat, 47g carbohydrate,
21mg cholesterol, 6g dietary fiber, 291mg sodium

Gingered Carrot Soup

Preparation time: 20 minutes (plus 1 hour cooking time)

This pureed soup is especially good with a vegetable salad. If you like a little heat, add a dash or two of hot pepper sauce before you purée.

2 tablespoons olive oil
1 small onion, finely chopped
3 tablespoons freshly grated ginger
5 carrots, chopped
6 cups vegetable broth
$^1/_2$ teaspoon salt
$^1/_2$ teaspoon pepper
1 tablespoon chopped fresh dill or 1 teaspoon dried

Heat oil in a pot and add onion. Cook over low heat until soft, about 8 minutes. Add ginger and sauté another minute or two. Add carrots and broth, increase heat and simmer, covered, for an hour, until carrots are tender. Purée soup in a blender or food processor, stir in salt, pepper, and dill.

Serves 4

Each Serving Provides:
136 calories, 2g protein, 7g fat, 16g carbohydrate,
0mg cholesterol, 4g dietary fiber, 315mg sodium

Gouda Vegetable Soup

Preparation time: 35 minutes

This soup is a complete meal with bread and cheese. I prefer
Yukon Gold potatoes when I make it, but any potato will do.

3 tablespoons oil
1 onion, finely chopped
3 stalks celery, sliced
2 carrots, peeled and sliced
4 Yukon gold or red potatoes, peeled and diced
1 1/2 cups broccoli florets
6 cups vegetable broth or water
1/2 red pepper, finely chopped
1 zucchini, diced
1 teaspoon dried thyme
1 teaspoon dried basil
12 pieces of bread from a baguette (or other bread),
    toasted
1/4 pound grated Gouda cheese

In a pot, heat oil and sauté onion, celery, and carrots 5 minutes. Add potatoes, broccoli, and broth, simmer 20 minutes.
Stir in pepper, zucchini, thyme, and basil, simmer 6 to 7 minutes more. Ladle soup into 6 bowls and add two pieces of
bread to each. Top with grated cheese. Place under a broiler
for a minute or two to melt the cheese, then serve.

Serves 6

Each Serving Provides:
302 calories, 11g protein, 13g fat, 37g carbohydrate,
21mg cholesterol, 6g dietary fiber, 271mg sodium

Salads

*W*estern Oregon winters may be bleak, but the springs are filled with windswept clouds coming off the Pacific and summers are nearly perfect, when rain is rare and humidity almost nonexistent during 80-degree days. The extensive selection of Willamette Valley fruits and vegetables, and the close proximity of farms to the cities here, make wonderful salads easy and quick summer meals.

Several of these salads will serve as a complete, light dinner with bread. Or try mixing and matching, making what I call a 3-course dinner plate — 3 different salads served together.

Raw vegetables often have higher nutrient value than cooked ones so a dinner of salads can be healthful, colorful, and delicious. Many of these salads are substantial as well, more so when you mix and match them.

Simple Vegetable Salad

Preparation time: 20 minutes

This simple salad is good for your health, goes well with many foods, or works as a light dinner or picnic on its own, served with bread.

1 carrot, julienned
2 tomatoes, chopped
1 cup cooked beans, white or black
1/2 sweet onion, minced
1 zucchini, julienned
1 cup green beans (1/2-inch pieces)
10 to 12 fresh basil leaves, chopped
2 tablespoons extra-virgin olive oil
1 tablespoon red wine vinegar
1/2 teaspoon chopped fresh thyme or 1/4 teaspoon dried
1 tablespoon chopped fresh parsley
Grated Parmesan cheese (optional)

Combine vegetables and basil in a bowl. Combine remaining ingredients except the cheese and whisk well; toss with vegetables. Top with cheese if desired.

Serves 4

Each Serving Provides:
169 calories, 6g protein, 8g fat, 22g carbohydrate,
0mg cholesterol, 3g dietary fiber, 247mg sodium

Perfect Summer Pasta Salad

Preparation time: 50 minutes

This refreshing salad is delightful for a summer dinner outside. Serve with some barbecued vegetables such as corn on the cob.

1 pound multi-colored seashell pasta
6 tablespoons extra-virgin olive oil
8 to 10 plum tomatoes, thickly sliced
1 stalk celery, thinly sliced
1 red bell pepper, seeded and diced
10 black olives, pitted and halved
8 ounces (2 cups) mozzarella cheese, cubed
Juice of 1 lemon (about 3 tablespoons)
1 teaspoon red wine vinegar
1 clove garlic, minced
2 teaspoons chopped fresh oregano or 1 teaspoon dried
$1/8$ teaspoon salt
$1/8$ teaspoon pepper

Cook pasta according to package directions, drain. Toss with 3 tablespoons of the olive oil and cool to room temperature. Add tomatoes, celery, pepper, olives, and cheese. Blend remaining ingredients together with the remaining 3 tablespoons olive oil and mix well. Pour over pasta and toss.

Serves 4

Each Serving Provides:
781 calories, 29g protein, 33g fat, 93g carbohydrate,
32mg cholesterol, 11g dietary fiber, 454mg sodium

Sweet Curry
Tropical Fruit Salad

Preparation time: 25 minutes

Make extra curry powder for this recipe and use the left-over powder for any other recipe that calls for curry, but add freshly grated ginger just before using (and include a little ground cayenne, too, which is omitted from this sweet curry). You could use a packaged curry powder to make this salad but it won't have the same sweet touch.

$^1/_4$ teaspoon *each* cardamom, turmeric, ground
    coriander, cumin
$^1/_8$ teaspoon *each* ground cloves, nutmeg
$^1/_2$ teaspoon sweet paprika
1 tablespoon grated fresh ginger
$^1/_2$ cup lemon or lime juice
$^1/_2$ cup honey
$^1/_2$ cup yogurt
2 kiwis, peeled and sliced
2 bananas, peeled and sliced
1 navel orange, peeled and sliced
2 mangoes or papayas, peeled and cut into pieces
1 small pineapple, peeled and cut into pieces

Combine ground spices to make a curry powder. Take 1 teaspoon of curry powder and place in a skillet over low heat and warm until aromatic, about a minute or two.

Remove to a bowl, add ginger, lemon or lime juice and mix. Stir in the honey and yogurt. Mix fruit in a bowl, then combine with dressing. Serve chilled or at room temperature.

Serves 4 to 6

Each Serving Provides:
259 calories, 3g protein, 1g fat, 65g carbohydrate,
1mg cholesterol, 5g dietary fiber, 19mg sodium

Warm Ravioli Salad

Preparation time: 25 minutes

With so many good ravioli products available in supermarkets and specialty stores nowadays, this dish is a great
way to let the cheese and pasta taste shine. A good balsamic vinegar gives it just a little bite. Serve with a vegetable salad.

4 tablespoons olive oil
1 onion, finely chopped
1 clove garlic, minced
5 bell peppers, a mix of green, yellow, and red,
    seeded and diced
1 pound fresh or frozen cheese ravioli
$1/4$ cup pine nuts (best if toasted for a few minutes in
    a 350° oven)
$1/2$ teaspoon chopped fresh thyme or $1/4$ teaspoon dried
2 tablespoons balsamic vinegar
$1/4$ teaspoon pepper

Heat oil and sauté onion, garlic, and peppers over low
heat 7 to 8 minutes. Meanwhile, cook ravioli according to
package instructions. Add pine nuts to the onion mixture
and remove from heat. Drain ravioli and combine all
ingredients.

Serves 4

Each Serving Provides:
*496 calories, 21g protein, 24g fat, 55g carbohydrate,
0mg cholesterol, 6g dietary fiber, 683mg sodium*

Corn & Sweet Pepper Pasta Salad

Preparation time: 25 minutes

This light pasta dish features a Dijon-style dressing that is great with fresh corn. It makes a colorful main dish or side dish, and is a favorite when we have a "3-Salad Dinner"—pasta, green, and vegetable.

10 ounces shell pasta or hollow pasta such as penne
   (about 4 cups dry)
2 cups cooked corn kernels, fresh (cut from 4 ears)
   or frozen
1 red bell pepper, seeded and julienned
1 green bell pepper, seeded and julienned
1 sweet onion, minced
1/2 zucchini, diced
2/3 cup extra-virgin olive oil
1/4 cup red wine vinegar
1 clove garlic, minced
2 teaspoons Dijon mustard
2 tablespoons minced parsley
1 teaspoon dried oregano

Cook pasta according to package directions. Drain and rinse with cold water to stop cooking. Toss pasta with corn, peppers, onion, and zucchini. In a separate bowl, combine remaining ingredients well, then toss with pasta. Serve warm or cold.

Serves 4

Each Serving Provides:
676 calories, 12g protein, 38g fat, 76g carbohydrate,
0mg cholesterol, 9g dietary fiber, 40mg sodium

Autumn Salad

Preparation time: 20 minutes

This hearty mix is welcome in the early fall, when tomatoes are still at their best. Serve with bread for dinner, or add a simple soup.

4 red or Yukon gold potatoes, peeled and cubed
$^{1}/_{2}$ pound green beans (2 cups), trimmed and sliced
2 tomatoes, sliced
$^{3}/_{4}$ cup garbanzo beans, drained
$^{1}/_{2}$ sweet onion, halved and thinly sliced
$^{1}/_{2}$ cup extra-virgin olive oil
3 tablespoons red wine vinegar
$^{1}/_{4}$ teaspoon pepper
1 teaspoon minced fresh parsley
$^{1}/_{2}$ teaspoon chopped fresh rosemary or $^{1}/_{4}$ teaspoon dried

Steam or microwave potatoes and green beans until just tender. Combine with tomatoes, garbanzo beans, and onion. Combine remaining ingredients in a small bowl and toss with the salad.

Serves 4

Each Serving Provides:
455 calories, 7g protein, 28g fat, 48g carbohydrate,
0mg cholesterol, 6g dietary fiber, 151mg sodium

Jasmine Rice Salad
with Ginger Dressing

Preparation time: 50 minutes

Jasmine rice can be difficult to find in stores, so this is a make-your-own version. The ginger goes nicely with the floral flavor of the rice.

1 jasmine tea bag
1 cup basmati or long-grain rice
1 cup fresh or frozen peas
1 carrot, thinly sliced
1/4 cup vegetable oil
2 tablespoons sesame oil
1/3 cup rice vinegar
1 1/2 teaspoons freshly grated ginger

Steep tea in a saucepan filled with 2 cups boiling water for 4 minutes. Discard bag, bring water to boil, and add rice. Cover, reduce heat to low, and simmer 15 to 17 minutes, or until water is absorbed. Uncover and cool.

    Steam or microwave peas until just tender. Cool, then toss with room temperature rice and carrots. Combine remaining ingredients in a bowl, toss well with rice mixture to coat. Serve at room temperature or chilled.

Serves 4

Each Serving Provides:
393 calories, 6g protein, 21g fat, 45g carbohydrate,
0mg cholesterol, 2g dietary fiber, 47mg sodium

Asian Pasta Salad

Preparation time: 20 minutes

Here is another salad that works as a complete meal. You might want to check your supermarket and experiment with thin Chinese noodles. I serve something simple on the side, such as Gingered Slaw (page 59).

8 ounces angel hair or other thin pasta
$^1/_4$ cup vegetable oil
2 tablespoons sesame oil
$1^1/_2$ tablespoons freshly grated ginger
1 teaspoon soy sauce
$^1/_8$ teaspoon red pepper flakes
1 small clove garlic, minced
1 teaspoon rice vinegar
$^1/_2$ teaspoon sugar
1 teaspoon lemon juice
3 scallions, sliced
$^1/_2$ cucumber, cubed
$^1/_2$ cup chopped cilantro
$^1/_2$ bell pepper, red or green, seeded and julienned

Cook pasta according to package directions, drain. Combine oils, ginger, soy sauce, red pepper flakes, garlic, vinegar, sugar, and lemon juice in a bowl and mix well.

Toss cooked pasta with scallions, cucumber, cilantro, and bell pepper. Add dressing and toss well.

Serves 4

Each Serving Provides:
425 calories, 8g protein, 22g fat, 49g carbohydrate,
0mg cholesterol, 3g dietary fiber, 96mg sodium

Spicy Potato-Jicama Salad

Preparation time: 40 minutes (plus 90 minutes chilling time)

A great summer salad, combining the sweet crunchy taste of jicama with hearty summer vegetables. Jicama, which tastes like a cross between an apple and a potato, is good in many potato salad recipes.

$2^{1}/_{2}$ pounds new or red potatoes
3 tablespoons olive oil
1 tablespoon white wine vinegar
1 small jicama, peeled and cut into matchsticks
$^{1}/_{2}$ cup mayonnaise
$^{1}/_{2}$ cup sour cream
1 teaspoon red pepper flakes
1 teaspoon dried basil
$^{1}/_{2}$ small red onion, halved and thinly sliced
$^{1}/_{2}$ bell pepper, red, yellow, or green, seeded and
    julienned

Place potatoes in a pan of boiling water and boil until just tender, but not falling apart. Rinse with cold water, cut into wedges. Add olive oil, vinegar, and jicama to potatoes and mix. Refrigerate until cold (about 90 minutes).

In a separate bowl, combine mayonnaise and sour cream. Add red pepper flakes and basil. Remove potato mixture from refrigerator and add onion and sweet pepper. Combine well with dressing. Serve at room temperature or cold.

Serves 4

Each Serving Provides:
595 calories, 7g protein, 36g fat, 64g carbohydrate,
28mg cholesterol, 5g dietary fiber, 185mg sodium

Today's Salad

Preparation time: 20 minutes

The day I perfected a sage and garlic pasta (page 84), I made quite a bit. We had leftovers the next night and I wanted a salad, so I made one with what was on hand. "What is it?" my boys asked, getting ready to mention all the salad ingredients they preferred not to eat. "Today's Salad," I replied. It's become one of my favorites.

$^1/_2$ sweet onion, thinly sliced
2 zucchinis, thinly sliced
$1^1/_2$ cups garbanzo beans, drained
1 red bell pepper, seeded and julienned
$^3/_4$ cup feta cheese
$^1/_4$ cup extra-virgin olive oil
3 tablespoons red wine vinegar
2 teaspoons lemon juice
2 teaspoons chopped fresh parsley
$^1/_2$ teaspoon dried oregano

If the onion isn't at the peak of sweetness, place slices in cold water for 20 minutes or so. Drain and toss with zucchinis, garbanzo beans, and red pepper. Crumble feta cheese on top. Mix remaining ingredients well in a small bowl, then toss with salad.

Serves 4

Each Serving Provides:
323 calories, 10g protein, 19g fat, 30g carbohydrate,
19mg cholesterol, 7g dietary fiber, 426mg sodium

Gingered Slaw

Preparation time: 15 minutes

This is a quick, colorful salad. Serve with a rice salad or pasta salad and bread for a healthful, fast dinner.

1 small cabbage, shredded
1 red bell pepper, seeded and julienned
2 tablespoons vegetable oil
1 tablespoon freshly grated ginger
2 tablespoons rice vinegar

Toss cabbage and pepper in a bowl. Combine oil, vinegar, and ginger in a separate bowl. Mix well and toss with cabbage mixture.

Serves 4

Each Serving Provides:
116 calories, 3g protein, 7g fat, 13g carbohydrate,
0mg cholesterol, 4g dietary fiber, 36mg sodium

Summer Tomatoes with Parsley

Preparation time: 15 minutes

The sweetness of ripe summer tomatoes matched with
slightly bitter parsley and a simple pungent dressing
makes a beautiful, delicious, quick addition to a summer
meal. A regular feature in our home.

1 to 2 cloves garlic
$^1/_2$ cup extra-virgin olive oil
3 tablespoons wine vinegar
$^1/_4$ teaspoon pepper
$^1/_4$ teaspoon salt
3 to 4 cups packed fresh parsley, chopped
$^1/_2$ cup grated Parmesan cheese
4 medium vine-ripened tomatoes, sliced

Process garlic, olive oil, vinegar, pepper, and salt in a
blender, or shake in a covered jar. Pour dressing over
parsley. Add Parmesan cheese and mix well. Put tomato
slices in a glass bowl. Add parsley mixture, toss well.

Serves 4

Each Serving Provides:
329 calories, 6g protein, 31g fat, 10g carbohydrate,
8mg cholesterol, 3g dietary fiber, 354mg sodium

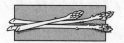

Pasta & Pizza

*T*he variety of pastas available in supermarkets continues to grow. Periodically I walk the pasta section and resupply my pantry; I like to have a wide range of dried pasta on hand so I can readily cook or create different pasta dishes.

Feel free to substitute other pastas for those in the recipes here. As a rule, for thin sauces look for noodles with ridges to catch the sauce. Cream sauces often benefit from a hollow pasta, while olive oil and heavy sauces are good with flat pastas.

Most of the recipes suggest you cook the pasta according to package directions then begin the sauce or other ingredients. Keep in mind that pasta should be prepared *al dente* every time — tender but chewy, not soft and mushy. When I cook pasta I take a sample out and bite into it a couple of minutes before the recommended time.

Mediterranean Macaroni

Preparation time: 15 minutes (plus 20 minutes baking time)

This twist on macaroni and cheese has three kinds of cheeses together with the color and sweetness of bell pepper. It's quick and easy too.

$^{1}/_{2}$ pound macaroni
1 tablespoon olive oil
$^{1}/_{4}$ onion, finely chopped
1 red or green bell pepper, seeded and diced
$^{1}/_{2}$ cup feta cheese, crumbled
$^{3}/_{4}$ cup grated Parmesan cheese
$^{3}/_{4}$ cup ricotta cheese
1 teaspoon dried dill
$^{1}/_{2}$ teaspoon pepper
1 egg
$^{1}/_{2}$ cup milk

Preheat oven to 350°. Cook macaroni according to package directions. Meanwhile, heat oil and sauté onion and bell pepper until soft, 7 to 8 minutes. Toss cooked macaroni with onion mixture, cheeses, dill, and pepper. Beat the egg and combine with milk, then stir into macaroni, mixing well. Pour into a lightly greased pan. Bake 20 minutes.

Serves 4

Each Serving Provides:
487 calories, 26g protein, 21g fat, 48g carbohydrate,
118mg cholesterol, 4g dietary fiber, 677mg sodium

Pasta with Raw Vegetables

Preparation time: 15 minutes

This quick dinner is good for your health and makes a very attractive plate. If you have it on hand, a light and fruity oil goes best with this dish. Make sure the pasta is coated well with olive oil before adding the vegetables.

1 pound penne or other hollow pasta
$^{1}/_{2}$ cup extra-virgin olive oil
$^{1}/_{2}$ red bell pepper, seeded and finely chopped
$^{1}/_{2}$ green bell pepper, seeded and finely chopped
$^{1}/_{2}$ sweet onion, finely chopped
1 tomato, cored and finely chopped
1 carrot, peeled and finely chopped
2 cups fresh basil, torn into pieces
Pepper
Grated Parmesan cheese

Cook pasta according to package directions, drain. Toss pasta with warmed olive oil. Top with vegetables and basil and toss. Serve with pepper and Parmesan to taste.

Serves 4

Each Serving Provides:
667 calories, 15g protein, 29g fat, 87g carbohydrate,
0mg cholesterol, 10g dietary fiber, 13mg sodium

Mexican Pizza

Preparation time: 20 minutes (plus 20 minutes soaking time for peppers)

Soaking the jalapeños reduces the heat. If you like your sauce spicier, don't seed the peppers.

1 ready-to-bake pizza crust, focaccia, or 6-inch slices
   of French bread cut from a baguette
3 to 4 tablespoons olive oil
2 jalapeños
4 tablespoons vegetable oil
1 red onion, thinly sliced
⅓ cup grated cheddar cheese
⅓ cup grated jack cheese
1 Anaheim pepper, seeded and dried, thinly sliced
1 teaspoon dried oregano
1 to 2 tablespoons chopped cilantro

Preheat oven to 400°. Rub the crust or bread with olive oil. Pour boiling water over jalapeños to cover and let sit 15 to 20 minutes, until softened. Seed jalapeños, then combine with vegetable oil in a food processor or chop finely and use a mortar and pestle to make a paste. Spread on the bread, then top with onion.

Combine cheeses and put on pizza. Lay Anaheim strips on top, sprinkle with oregano. Bake 10 to 12 minutes. Sprinkle cilantro on top.

Serves 4

Each Serving Provides:
502 calories, 12g protein, 32g fat, 41g carbohydrate,
17mg cholesterol, 3g dietary fiber, 452mg sodium

Potato Gnocchi with Herbed Tomato Sauce

Preparation time: 2¹/₂ hours

This dish is not particularly difficult to make; it takes time to prepare and cook, but it's worth the effort. Gnocchi is wonderful comfort food and great with a salad.

1 can (15 ounces) tomatoes with juice
2 cloves garlic, minced
¹/₂ small onion, minced
1 tablespoon chopped fresh oregano or 1 teaspoon dried
1¹/₂ teaspoons dried thyme
1¹/₂ teaspoons dried marjoram
1 bay leaf
1¹/₂ teaspoons pepper
¹/₂ cup dry red wine
¹/₄ cup torn fresh basil or ¹/₈ cup dried
¹/₄ cup chopped fresh parsley
2 tablespoons butter or oil
1 pound Yukon gold or other potatoes, unpeeled
1 egg
1 teaspoon salt
1³/₄ cups flour, plus a little more for kneading
Grated Parmesan cheese (optional)

Combine tomatoes, garlic, onion, oregano, thyme, marjoram, bay leaf, and pepper in a large pot and bring to a boil. Reduce heat and simmer, stirring occasionally, for 1 hour. Add wine, basil, and parsley and cook 30 minutes longer. Remove bay leaf.

Meanwhile, use 1 tablespoon butter or oil to lightly coat a 9 x 13-inch baking dish. Cut potatoes into 1-inch chunks. Boil in water to cover until soft, about 25 minutes.

Drain potatoes and place in a food processor fitted with a steel blade. Start processing, then add egg, the remaining 1 tablespoon butter or oil, and salt and mix until creamy.

Remove the potato mixture to a bowl and add $^1\!/_4$ cup of flour at a time, mixing well, turning the batter into dough. Turn it out on a floured surface and knead a few minutes, adding flour as needed.

Fill a large saucepan with water and begin to heat. Preheat oven to 300°. Tear off a palm-sized ball of dough, dust it in flour, and roll into a rope about an inch in diameter. Cut the rope into 1-inch pieces, repeating the process with remaining dough.

When water reaches a boil add as many pieces of dough as you can without crowding. Cover and simmer 40 minutes. Remove, place in baking dish, then add the next batch of dough to the water.

Bake 30 minutes until just brown. Toss with 1 cup or more sauce, as desired, then top with Parmesan.

Serves 4 to 6

Each Serving Provides:
270 calories, 6g protein, 6g fat, 47g carbohydrate,
47mg cholesterol, 3g dietary fiber, 542mg sodium

Middle Eastern Spaghetti

Preparation time: 15 minutes

A simple dish of the Middle East, with variations including meat, cheese, or eggs depending on the country. Enjoy this with a cucumber and dill salad.

12 ounces spaghetti
2 cups lowfat yogurt
1 clove garlic, minced
1 cup feta or other Middle Eastern cheese
$1/8$ cup minced parsley
2 tablespoons olive oil

Cook spaghetti according to package directions, drain. Combine yogurt, garlic, cheese, and parsley and set aside. Toss the cooked spaghetti with olive oil, then add yogurt mixture and toss again.

Serves 4

Each Serving Provides:
541 calories, 21g protein, 16g fat, 77g carbohydrate,
32mg cholesterol, 4g dietary fiber, 398mg sodium

Spaghettini with Salsa

Preparation time: 20 minutes

This quick dish with its uncooked sauce is great when fresh tomatoes are at their best. The sauce actually gets cooked — by the hot pasta.

7 ripe tomatoes, seeded and chopped, with juice
4 cloves garlic, minced
5 tablespoons chopped fresh basil
$^1/_2$ teaspoon minced fresh oregano or $^1/_4$ teaspoon dried
$^1/_2$ cup extra-virgin olive oil
3 scallions, minced
$^1/_4$ teaspoon pepper
1 pound spaghettini or other thin pasta
Grated Parmesan cheese (optional)

Combine all ingredients except pasta and cheese in a bowl. Toss well and set aside. Cook pasta according to package directions, drain, then return to the hot pan. Combine with sauce, top with Parmesan, if desired, and serve.

Serves 4

Each Serving Provides:
732 calories, 17g protein, 30g fat, 101g carbohydrate,
0mg cholesterol, 8g dietary fiber, 23mg sodium

Greek Pasta

Preparation time: 20 minutes

This quick dish is a blend of the traditional Greek tastes of feta and olives.

30 to 35 fresh basil leaves
1 cup crumbled feta cheese
2 cloves garlic, minced
$1/4$ cup yogurt
$1/2$ cup sour cream
$1/4$ teaspoon pepper
2 tablespoons extra-virgin olive oil
4 to 5 mushrooms, sliced
1 red bell pepper, seeded and diced
$1/2$ cup pitted and halved calamata olives
3 cherry tomatoes, quartered
1 pound shell pasta

Process basil, feta, garlic, yogurt, sour cream, and pepper until smooth. Heat oil in a skillet and sauté mushrooms and bell pepper for 5 minutes. Remove to a bowl and toss with the olives and tomatoes. Cook the pasta according to package directions, drain, and combine with the vegetables. Toss with sauce and serve.

Serves 4

Each Serving Provides:
642 calories, 20g protein, 24g fat, 88g carbohydrate,
38mg cholesterol, 9g dietary fiber, 793mg sodium

Rigatoni with Olives & Hot Pepper

Preparation time: 35 minutes

This spicy sauce is also good (minus the capers) on pizza.
Serve with a green salad.

2 tablespoons olive oil
6 roma tomatoes, chopped
3 tablespoons minced fresh basil or 1 tablespoon dried
1 clove garlic, minced
1 tablespoon seeded and minced jalapeño
8 pitted calamata olives, halved
1 tablespoon drained capers
$1/2$ teaspoon dried oregano
1 pound rigatoni

Put 1 tablespoon oil in a saucepan with tomatoes and
bring to a boil. Cover and simmer 8 to 9 minutes, until
soft. Remove to a blender or food processor, add basil,
and purée. Reserve. Heat remaining 1 tablespoon oil, add
garlic and jalapeño, and stir 3 to 4 minutes. Add tomato
purée and mix. Add olives, capers, and oregano and cook,
covered, 15 minutes, stirring frequently. Cook the pasta
according to package directions, drain. Toss with sauce
and serve.

Serves 4

Each Serving Provides:
504 calories, 15g protein, 11g fat, 88g carbohydrate,
0mg cholesterol, 10g dietary fiber, 190mg sodium

Pasta Puttanesca

Preparation time: 40 minutes (plus 1 hour, 20 minutes cooking time)

This is an Italian classic, but made this time without the anchovies. I like this hearty dish with bread and wine.

1 pound spaghetti or other pasta
12 fresh, peeled tomatoes with juice (see page 14) or
    2 cans (28 ounces *each*) chopped tomatoes
$1/3$ cup extra-virgin olive oil
1 onion, finely chopped
8 cloves garlic, minced
$1/4$ cup chopped fresh parsley
1 carrot, grated
3 tablespoons chopped fresh oregano or $1^1/2$ table-
    spoons dried
3 tablespoons chopped fresh basil or $1^1/2$ tablespoons
    dried
$2/3$ cup red wine
2 tablespoons drained capers
1 cup pitted and sliced black olives, preferably cala-
    mata
Grated Parmesan cheese (optional)

Purée half the tomatoes and set aside. Heat oil in a skillet and add onion. Sauté 3 to 4 minutes, then add garlic and sauté 1 minute more. Add parsley, carrot, oregano, and basil and cook another minute or two. Add the remaining half of the tomatoes and tomato purée and bring to a boil. Cook down 5 minutes, stirring, then cover and simmer for an hour, stirring occasionally. Add the red wine, capers, and olives and simmer, uncovered, 20 minutes longer. Meanwhile, cook pasta according to package directions, drain. Toss sauce with pasta and top with Parmesan cheese, if desired.

Serves 4

Each Serving Provides:
853 calories, 21g protein, 32g fat, 122g carbohydrate, 0mg cholesterol, 13g dietary fiber, 1052mg sodium

Potato Lasagna

Preparation time: 45 minutes (plus 50 minutes baking time)

Here's a potato and noodle mixture with both tomato and pesto sauces. It's a great leftover, too.

5 tablespoons plus $^{1}/_{4}$ cup extra-virgin olive oil
4 cloves garlic
$^{1}/_{2}$ onion, chopped
1 can (15 ounces) tomatoes with juice
$^{1}/_{2}$ teaspoon dried oregano
$^{1}/_{2}$ teaspoon dried basil
$^{1}/_{2}$ teaspoon pepper
18 to 20 fresh basil leaves
$^{1}/_{4}$ cup pine nuts
$^{2}/_{3}$ cup grated Romano or Parmesan cheese
2 to 3 potatoes, thinly sliced
1 bunch fresh spinach or 1 package (10 ounces)
    frozen
$^{1}/_{2}$ pound lasagna noodles, cooked
1 package (15 ounces) ricotta cheese
$^{1}/_{2}$ pound mozzarella cheese, sliced

To make the tomato sauce: Mix 2 tablespoons olive oil with 2 cloves garlic and onion in a saucepan, to coat. Turn heat to medium and sauté 6 to 7 minutes. Add tomatoes with their juice, and the oregano, dried basil, and pepper. Bring to a boil and simmer 20 minutes. Reserve 2 cups of sauce for this dish and save the rest for pasta or pizza.

To make the pesto: Place fresh basil leaves in blender along with the remaining 2 cloves garlic, pine nuts, $^{1}/_{3}$ cup grated Romano or Parmesan, and $^{1}/_{4}$ cup or more olive oil. Purée until smooth. Reserve $^1/_2$ cup pesto for this dish, saving the rest for pasta or another dish.

Preheat oven to 350°. Steam potatoes until just tender, about 10 minutes. Steam the spinach 4 to 5 minutes, or cook frozen spinach according to package directions and squeeze out excess liquid.

Layer half the potatoes in a greased 9x13-inch baking dish, top with noodles, spinach, and half *each* of the ricotta, tomato sauce, pesto, and mozzarella. Repeat, topping with remaining $^1/_3$ cup Romano or Parmesan cheese and 3 tablespoons olive oil. Bake, covered, 25 minutes, then uncovered another 20 to 30 minutes.

Serves 4 to 6

Each Serving Provides:
682 calories, 34g protein, 39g fat, 52g carbohydrate,
51mg cholesterol, 4g dietary fiber, 859mg sodium

Red Pepper & Feta Calzone

Preparation time: 30 minutes (using refrigerated dough)

I started making these quick calzones (using refrigerated dough from the store) with meat and graduated to this vegetarian dish. This can be made in 30 minutes and is always filling and well received. While they bake you can make a green salad.

2 tablespoons extra-virgin olive oil
$^1/_2$ onion, chopped
2 cloves garlic, minced
1 can (15 ounces) tomatoes with juice
1 tablespoon chopped fresh basil or 1 teaspoon dried
$^1/_2$ teaspoon dried dill
1 small zucchini, diced
$^1/_2$ cup feta cheese, grated or crumbled
1 roasted red bell pepper, seeded and diced, (see
    page 14)
1 cup grated mozzarella
Pizza dough (use refrigerated from store or fresh,
    page 10)

Preheat oven to 425°. Lightly oil a baking sheet. Heat 1 tablespoon olive oil in a skillet and sauté onion and garlic until onion is soft, about 5 minutes. Add tomatoes, basil, and dill, bring to a boil and simmer, stirring occasionally, 15 to 20 minutes. Place in a blender and purée, leaving some texture. Heat remaining 1 tablespoon oil and sauté zucchini until cooked, about 5 minutes. Remove to a bowl with a slotted spoon and mix well with the feta cheese, red pepper, and $^1/_2$ cup tomato sauce. Add mozzarella and mix well.

Spread pizza dough out into a 12 x 12-inch square. Cut into four equal pieces and place $^1/_4$ of the filling in each square. Pull the dough over the top, in a triangle, and poke holes in the top with a fork to vent. Place on baking sheet and bake 15 minutes, until brown. Pour additional sauce as desired on top and serve.

Makes 4 calzones

Each Serving Provides:
397 calories, 17g protein, 17g fat, 44g carbohydrate,
29mg cholesterol, 3g dietary fiber, 1066mg sodium

Pasta Pesto Primavera

Preparation time: 20 minutes

The color of this dish makes it a beautiful main course for guests, yet it is easy enough to make for family. The pesto is a parsley-walnut mix, combined with the traditional basil.

10 fresh basil leaves
2 to 3 small parsley sprigs
1 clove garlic
4 tablespoons extra-virgin olive oil
1/4 cup walnuts
4 spears asparagus, trimmed and cut into 1 1/2" pieces
1 small zucchini, diced
3 mushrooms, sliced
1 bell pepper, seeded and cut into strips
2 cups chopped broccoli florets
1/2 stalk celery, sliced
1 pound thin pasta
3 tablespoons pine nuts, roasted
Grated Parmesan cheese (optional)

Preheat oven to 375°. Place the basil, parsley, garlic, olive oil, and walnuts in a blender or food processor and purée. Set aside.

   In a skillet, add 1/3 cup water and the asparagus, zucchini, mushrooms, pepper, broccoli, and celery and bring to a boil. Cover and cook over medium heat 3 minutes then remove the lid and cook until liquid is evaporated.

Cook pasta according to package directions, drain. Toss pesto mixture with the vegetables, then toss all with pasta. Sprinkle on pine nuts and add Parmesan cheese if desired.

Serves 4

Each Serving Provides:
694 calories, 22g protein, 24g fat, 101g carbohydrate,
0mg cholesterol, 10g dietary fiber, 36mg sodium

Zucchini & Pepper Pasta

Preparation time: 20 minutes

This simple, quick, healthful, and colorful pasta has uncomplicated flavors which go well with light or sweet breads.

4 tablespoons extra-virgin olive oil
1/2 onion, chopped
2 cloves garlic, minced
4 zucchinis, sliced
2 carrots, sliced
1 red bell pepper, seeded and julienned
1 tablespoon dried oregano
12 ounces fettucine
2 tablespoons lemon juice

Heat 2 tablespoons oil in skillet, add onion, and sauté 5 minutes over medium heat. Add garlic, sauté another minute, then add zucchini, carrots, bell pepper, and oregano. Sauté 10 minutes, stirring frequently.

Cook pasta according to package directions. Drain and toss with lemon juice. Add vegetable mixture to the pasta, toss well, and serve.

Serves 4

Each Serving Provides:
518 calories, 15g protein, 16g fat, 81g carbohydrate,
0mg cholesterol, 8g dietary fiber, 23mg sodium

Mediterranean Orzo

Preparation time: 20 minutes

Orzo looks like rice, but has a softer, fuller texture. It's a nice substitute in some rice recipes. Here it is paired with flavors of the Mediterranean.

$^1/_2$ sweet onion, chopped
4 cloves garlic, minced
$^1/_2$ red bell pepper, seeded and diced
4 tablespoons extra-virgin olive oil
2 tomatoes, seeded and diced
2 tablespoons drained capers (optional)
$1^1/_2$ teaspoons chopped fresh oregano or $^1/_2$ teaspoon dried
$^1/_2$ teaspoon salt
$^1/_2$ teaspoon pepper
2 teaspoons chopped fresh basil or 1 teaspoon dried
1 pound orzo
1 cup feta cheese

In a cold skillet, combine the onion, garlic, and bell pepper in 2 tablespoons oil. Place over medium heat and sauté just 3 to 4 minutes so the pepper and onion retain some crispness. Add tomatoes and capers and just heat through, then remove from heat. Add the oregano, salt, pepper, and basil. Meanwhile, cook orzo according to package directions, drain. Toss vegetables with pasta amd remaining 2 tablespoons oil, then stir in crumbled feta.

Serves 4

Each Serving Provides:
646 calories, 19g protein, 22g fat, 91g carbohydrate,
25mg cholesterol, 5g dietary fiber, 589mg sodium

Vegetarian Lasagna

Preparation time: 25 minutes (plus 40 minutes baking time)

Lasagna is a favorite food of almost everyone, and with the lowfat cheeses available it doesn't have to be loaded with fat. Enjoy with a salad and vinaigrette.

1 tablespoon olive oil
1/2 onion, finely chopped
2 cloves garlic, minced
6 tomatoes, chopped
1 teaspoon dried oregano
2 tablespoons minced fresh basil or 2 teaspoons dried
1/4 teaspoon pepper
1/2 pound lasagna noodles, cooked
15 ounces ricotta cheese
2 cups (8 ounces) grated mozzarella
1/2 cup grated Parmesan cheese
1 zucchini, diced
5 to 6 mushrooms, sliced and then halved
3 cups chopped fresh spinach

Preheat oven to 350°. Heat oil in a saucepan and sauté onion and garlic 5 minutes. Purée the tomatoes, then add onion and garlic, along with the oregano, basil, and pepper. Simmer 15 minutes, remove from heat, and spoon out enough sauce to cover the bottom of a 13 x 9-inch baking dish. Place a layer of lasagna noodles then top with $1/3$ of the remaining ingredients, then cover with sauce. Repeat for two more layers, ending with sauce. Bake until hot, about 40 minutes.

Serves 4 to 6

Each Serving Provides:
488 calories, 31g protein, 15g fat, 59g carbohydrate, 37mg cholesterol, 4g dietary fiber, 686mg sodium

Zagliatone with Sage & Garlic

Preparation time: 20 minutes

This is a splurge recipe, one we might have cooked before we cut back on the fats. But, for the occasional off-the-diet treat, this is a wonderful sauce.

1 pound zagliatone, penne, or other hollow pasta
8 tablespoons butter (1 stick)
2 cloves garlic, minced
1 1/2 teaspoons dried sage
1/4 cup flour
1 1/2 cups milk
3/4 cup grated Parmesan cheese

Cook pasta according to package directions, drain. Melt butter in a saucepan over low heat and add garlic and sage. Stir to mix and heat 5 minutes. Add flour and stir, cooking 2 minutes. Add milk gradually, and stir 5 minutes. Mix in cheese and toss with the cooked pasta.

Serves 4

Each Serving Provides:
756 calories, 24g protein, 33g fat, 91g carbohydrate,
85mg cholesterol, 8g dietary fiber, 574mg sodium

Sweet Pepper & Pine Nut Pasta

Preparation time: 20 minutes

Sometimes the simpler the recipe the better. I like pasta tossed with good olive oil. Here I add red peppers (roasted if you like) and pine nuts.

1 pound linguine or other pasta
4 tablespoons extra-virgin olive oil
2 bell peppers, preferably red and yellow, seeded and diced
3 cloves garlic, minced
1/4 cup shredded fresh basil
1 teaspoon minced fresh thyme or 1/2 teaspoon dried
3 tablespoons pine nuts, toasted in a skillet over medium heat for 2 minutes
Grated Parmesan cheese(optional)

Cook pasta according to package directions, drain. Heat 2 tablespoons oil in a skillet, add the peppers and garlic. Sauté over low heat until peppers are softened, 8 to 10 minutes. Add basil, thyme, and remaining 2 tablespoons oil. Toss with cooked pasta, add pine nuts, and toss again. Sprinkle with Parmesan if desired.

Serves 4

Each Serving Provides:
615 calories, 17g protein, 20g fat, 94g carbohydrate,
0mg cholesterol, 6g dietary fiber, 4mg sodium

Spicy Fettuccine with Red Peppers & Mushrooms

Preparation time: 35 minutes

This is a hot pasta sauce so you might want something cool, like a chilled soup, to serve alongside it.

1 pound fettuccine
4 tablespoons extra-virgin olive oil
$1/2$ onion, diced
3 cloves garlic, minced
$1/8$ teaspoon red pepper flakes, or to taste
$1/8$ teaspoon ground cayenne
1 teaspoon chopped fresh oregano or $1/2$ teaspoon
    dried
3 tomatoes, peeled and chopped with juice
    or 1 can (28 ounces) with juice
2 tablespoons minced fresh parsley
1 bell pepper, seeded and julienned
4 to 5 mushrooms, sliced
Grated Parmesan cheese (optional)

Cook fettuccine according to package directions, drain. Combine 2 tablespoons olive oil, onion, garlic, red pepper flakes, cayenne, and oregano in a saucepan and sauté 6 minutes. Add tomatoes and bring to a boil. Reduce heat and simmer 20 minutes, stirring occasionally, then stir in parsley.

Meanwhile, heat remaining 2 tablespoons oil in a skillet and sauté pepper and mushrooms until just softened, 5 to 7 minutes. Toss pasta with pepper mixture, then with the sauce. Serve with Parmesan if desired.

Serves 4

Each Serving Provides:
608 calories, 17g protein, 16g fat, 99g carbohydrate,
0mg cholesterol, 7g dietary fiber, 15mg sodium

Penne with Pizza Sauce

Preparation time: 30 minutes

This is pizza in a bowl. You can add other "pizza top-
pings" you might like such as bell peppers or black olives.
If you like it spicy, add ¹/₂ teaspoon red pepper flakes in
place of the dill.

4 tablespoons extra-virgin olive oil
1 small onion, finely chopped
4 cloves garlic, minced
1 can (28 ounces) crushed tomatoes with juice
1 tablespoon dried dill
1 tablespoon dried thyme
2 bay leaves
1 pound penne or other hollow pasta
4 to 5 mushrooms, sliced
Grated Parmesan cheese (optional)

Place 3 tablespoons of oil along with the onion and garlic
in an unheated saucepan and stir to coat. Cook over mod-
erate-low heat until garlic just begins to turn golden (but
do not brown), 3 to 4 minutes. Add tomatoes and seasonings, bring to a boil, reduce heat, and simmer 20 minutes.
Discard bay leaves.

Meanwhile, cook pasta according to package directions, drain. Heat remaining 1 tablespoon oil and sauté mushrooms until just softened, 3 to 4 minutes. Add mushrooms to sauce, toss with pasta, and add cheese if desired.

Serves 4

Each Serving Provides:
*584 calories, 16g protein, 16g fat, 95g carbohydrate,
0mg cholesterol, 10g dietary fiber, 351mg sodium*

Linguine with Tomato Ricotta Cream

Preparation time: 25 minutes

The smoothness of the ricotta complements the tomato sauce in this pasta dish. Use any flat noodle you have handy.

1 pound linguine
3 tablespoons olive oil
6 fresh roma tomatoes, chopped
3 cloves garlic, minced
$1/4$ cup minced fresh basil
$1/2$ cup minced fresh parsley
2 teaspoons snipped fresh dill or 1 teaspoon dried
$1/2$ teaspoon salt
1 cup lowfat ricotta cheese
Grated Parmesan cheese (optional)

Cook pasta according to package directions, drain. Heat oil in a skillet and add tomatoes and garlic. Cook 3 minutes, then add basil, parsley, dill, and salt. Cook down, uncovered, 10 to 15 minutes. Remove from heat, stir in ricotta cheese. Toss with cooked pasta and serve with Parmesan cheese if desired.

Serves 4

Each Serving Provides:
655 calories, 26g protein, 18g fat, 99g carbohydrate,
25mg cholesterol, 7g dietary fiber, 325mg sodium

Vegetarian Bolognese

Preparation time: 30 minutes (plus 1 hour cooking time)

This comes to me from Carol Bartley, who is always very creative as she cooks vegetarian style from her Portland garden.

$^{1}/_{3}$ cup olive oil
6 cloves garlic, minced
1 small onion, minced
1 carrot, minced
1 large potato, grated
1 stalk celery, minced
1 cup chopped fresh parsley
$^{1}/_{4}$ cup water
6 to 7 fresh roma tomatoes or 1 can (28 ounces), drained
1 pound spaghetti

Heat oil and slowly sauté the garlic, onion, carrot, and celery until soft, about 10 minutes. Add potato and cook 15 minutes or until soft, stirring to keep from sticking. Add parsley and continue to cook 5 minutes more. Add water, stir, add the tomatoes. Cook slowly, stirring often, covering occasionally, for about an hour. Add a little more water if the sauce cooks down. Meanwhile, cook pasta according to package directions, drain. Toss pasta with sauce.

Serves 4

Each Serving Provides:
697 calories, 18g protein, 21g fat, 111g carbohydrate,
0mg cholesterol, 9g dietary fiber, 41mg sodium

Spaghetti with Fresh Basil & Tomato

Preparation time: 25 minutes

This basic sauce lets the taste of basil and tomato, that most natural of marriages, shine through. For tips on peeling tomatoes, see page 14.

1 pound spaghetti
2 tablespoons olive oil
3 cloves garlic, minced
4 roma tomatoes, peeled, seeded, and chopped,
    or 1 can (15 ounces) tomatoes, drained
1/3 cup chopped fresh parsley
1/2 cup chopped fresh basil
1/2 cup yogurt
2 cups (8 ounces) grated mozzarella
1/2 cup grated Parmesan cheese

Cook spaghetti according to package directions, drain. Heat olive oil and sauté garlic over low heat for 5 minutes. Add the tomatoes, parsley, and basil and bring to a boil. Reduce heat, stir in the yogurt, cooked spaghetti, and cheeses.

Serves 4

Each Serving Provides:
737 calories, 36g protein, 22g fat, 99g carbohydrate,
42mg cholesterol, 7g dietary fiber, 485mg sodium

Pasta with Nella's Red Sauce

Preparation time: 55 minutes (plus 25 minutes baking time)

This delicate sauce is best with a ribbed pasta, gemelli or zagliatone. It came to me by way of my friend Carol Bartley who credits Nella Bonifazi.

10 roma tomatoes, quartered
1 tablespoon olive oil
2 carrots, cut in half
1 onion, cut in half
3 cloves garlic, peeled and smashed
$^{1}/_{4}$ cup chopped fresh basil or 2 tablespoons dried
1 pound gemelli or other pasta
1 cup grated Romano cheese
1 cup grated Parmesan cheese

Over low heat, cook the tomatoes until liquified, about 20 minutes. Press through a food mill and put tomato sauce in a skillet with the oil, carrots, onion, and garlic. Simmer 30 minutes, discard vegetables and add basil, cook another 5 minutes.

Preheat oven to 325°. Meanwhile, cook the pasta halfway and drain. Stir cheeses into the tomato sauce to blend well, then mix in with the pasta. Place in a lightly oiled baking dish and bake, covered, 20 minutes. Remove cover and bake another 5 to 10 minutes until cooked through and bubbly.

Serves 4

Each Serving Provides:
698 calories, 34g protein, 18g fat, 102g carbohydrate,
36mg cholesterol, 8g dietary fiber, 636mg sodium

Spinach Gnocchi
with Rosemary Butter

Preparation time: 30 minutes (plus 4 hours refrigeration time)

These gnocchi are wonderful in a rosemary flavored butter. If that's too rich, a good tomato sauce will do.

1 bunch fresh spinach or 1 package (10 ounces),
    frozen
7 ounces (1³/₄ cup) grated mozzarella
3 tablespoons grated Parmesan cheese
5 tablespoons flour plus additional for dredging
3 eggs
6 tablespoons butter (optional)
1 sprig fresh rosemary (optional)
1 tablespoon olive oil

Wash and trim the spinach then steam until wilted, about 5 minutes; or cook frozen spinach according to package directions and squeeze out excess liquid. Purée spinach then add the cheeses and 5 tablespoons flour. Add one egg at a time, blending well. Refrigerate 4 hours or overnight, or place in the freezer until firm.

In a skillet melt the butter. Place the rosemary sprig in the butter and keep warm, stirring occasionally, while you make the gnocchi.

Form the cold dough into small tubes and dredge in flour. Shake off excess flour and drop several gnocchi into boiling water with olive oil and simmer about 9 minutes. Drain on paper towels, cover, and repeat with remaining dough.

Discard the rosemary sprig. Toss gnocchi with the rosemary butter and serve.

Serves 4

Each Serving Provides:
277 calories, 21g protein, 16g fat, 11g carbohydrate, 191mg cholesterol, 2g dietary fiber, 392mg sodium

Lemon Bowties
with Zucchini and Herbs

Preparation time: 25 minutes

This dish is much better with fresh herbs. It's an easy meal accompanied by fresh tomato slices or carrot sticks, and bread.

1 pound bowties (farfalle) or other pasta such as shells
1 zucchini, cut into matchsticks
1 tablespoon lemon zest
1 teaspoon lemon juice
1 tablespoon *each* minced fresh dill, parsley, basil, marjoram, thyme, or 1 1/2 teaspoons *each* dried
4 tablespoons extra-virgin olive oil
1/4 cup pine nuts, toasted
1/4 cup grated Parmesan cheese (optional)

Cook pasta according to package directions, drain. Blanch the zucchini slices by dropping into boiling water for 30 seconds, then drain. Combine the lemon zest, lemon juice, herbs, and olive oil in a bowl, add zucchini, and toss to coat. Add cooked pasta and toss again to coat. Sprinkle on pine nuts and add Parmesan cheese, if desired.

Serves 4

Each Serving Provides:
578 calories, 17g protein, 21g fat, 84g carbohydrate,
0mg cholesterol, 9g dietary fiber, 6mg sodium

Curried Noodles

Preparation time: 20 minutes

This is a mild curry, so even the kids will like it. You can substitute a good-quality curry powder for the first three lines of spices, if desired.

$1/4$ teaspoon *each* cardamom, turmeric, coriander, cumin
$1/8$ teaspoon *each* ground cloves, mace, cayenne
$1/2$ teaspoon sweet paprika
4 to 5 ounces angel hair or other thin pasta
1 tablespoon sesame oil
1 tablespoon vegetable oil
1 onion, halved and thinly sliced
1 red bell pepper, seeded and julienned
4 mushrooms, sliced
3 scallions, thinly sliced
1 tablespoon freshly grated ginger

Combine curry spices and set aside. Cook pasta according to package directions, drain. In a wok or large skillet, heat the oils until they sizzle slightly. Add onion and sauté 3 minutes. Add curry spices and stir another minute. Add bell pepper and mushrooms and sauté another 2 to 3 minutes, reduce heat, and add scallions, pasta, and ginger. Stir to mix well.

Serves 4

Each Serving Provides:
213 calories, 5g protein, 8g fat, 31g carbohydrate,
0mg cholesterol, 3g dietary fiber, 6mg sodium

Easy Ricotta & Spinach Cannelloni

Preparation time: 40 minutes

This easy dish is always a hit, and it's a complete meal. Be careful not to overfill the cannelloni since they expand during cooking. I serve it with a salad.

14 cannelloni tubes
2 tablespoons extra-virgin olive oil
1 small onion, chopped
2 cloves garlic, minced
3 tomatoes, peeled and chopped, with juice
    or 1 can (15 ounces)
$1/2$ teaspoon dried dill
$1/2$ teaspoon dried oregano
1 teaspoon dried basil
4 mushrooms, sliced
2 bunches fresh spinach, washed and chopped,
    or 2 packages (10 ounces *each*) frozen spinach
1 egg, beaten
15 ounces ricotta cheese
3 tablespoons grated Parmesan cheese

Preheat oven to 400°. Cook pasta according to package directions and drain. Combine olive oil with the onion and garlic in a saucepan to coat, then turn heat to medium-low and sauté until onion is soft, about 10 minutes. Add tomatoes, dill, oregano, and basil, bring to a boil, reduce heat and simmer 15 minutes, until sauce is cooked down. Add mushrooms and simmer 5 minutes more.

Meanwhile, steam the fresh spinach until just wilted, 4 to 5 minutes, or cook frozen spinach according to package directions and squeeze out excess liquid. Combine spinach, egg, and cheeses in a bowl and mix well. Fill cannelloni tubes with the mixture and place in a lightly oiled baking dish. Pour tomato sauce over filled cannelloni and bake 15 minutes.

Serves 4 to 6

Each Serving Provides:
479 calories, 23g protein, 11g fat, 74g carbohydrate,
48mg cholesterol, 7g dietary fiber, 450mg sodium

Ziti with Walnut Sauce

Preparation time: 10 minutes

Nothing is quicker than this simple purée of walnuts and oil, which kids usually like. Serve with sliced vegetables on the side.

1 pound ziti or other hollow pasta
4 cloves garlic, minced
1 cup chopped walnuts
$1/3$ cup extra-virgin olive oil
$1/3$ cup grated Parmesan cheese
$1/4$ cup or more hot water from pasta
$1/4$ cup fresh parsley, minced

Cook pasta according to package instructions. Drain, reserving a little water, and place in the hot pot. Place garlic, walnuts, oil, and cheese in a blender or food processor and process, leaving some texture. Add a little water, if needed, then toss with the pasta and warm over low heat. Top with parsley and serve.

Serves 4

Each Serving Provides:
774 calories, 21g protein, 40g fat, 87g carbohydrate,
5mg cholesterol, 10g dietary fiber, 138mg sodium

Angel Hair with Fennel & Basil

Preparation time: 20 minutes

Fennel is becoming more readily available in supermarket produce sections. Fresh fennel resists pressure and is firm to the touch. Here it's mixed in with pasta.

1 pound angel hair or other thin pasta
2 tablespoons extra-virgin olive oil
1 tablespoon butter
$^1/_2$ sweet onion, minced
1 clove garlic, minced
$^3/_4$ cup minced fresh fennel
$^1/_3$ cup minced fresh basil
$^1/_3$ cup minced fresh parsley
Grated Parmesan cheese (optional)

Cook pasta according to package directions, drain. Heat oil and butter in a skillet and sauté the onion and garlic until soft, about 7 minutes. Add fennel and sauté another 5 minutes. Combine basil and parsley, then add to skillet for 2 minutes, stirring constantly. Toss with pasta and serve with Parmesan if desired.

Serves 4

Each Serving Provides:
550 calories, 16g protein, 12g fat, 94g carbohydrate,
8mg cholesterol, 6g dietary fiber, 44mg sodium

Ziti with Marinated Tomatoes

Preparation time: 20 minutes (plus 2 hours marinating time)

This wonderful little meal can be readied in the morning before work (even the night before) in minutes. Then just cook the pasta, grate the cheese, and eat.

8 roma tomatoes, chopped
$^1/_2$ bell pepper, seeded and finely chopped
3 cloves garlic, minced
3 tablespoons chopped fresh basil or 1 tablespoon
    dried
$^2/_3$ cup extra-virgin olive oil
$^1/_2$ teaspoon dried thyme
1 tablespoon seeded and minced jalapeño (optional)
$^1/_2$ teaspoon salt
$^1/_2$ teaspoon pepper
$^1/_2$ cup (2 ounces) grated mozzarella cheese
$^1/_3$ cup ricotta cheese
1 pound ziti or other hollow pasta
Grated Parmesan cheese (optional)

Combine tomatoes, bell pepper, garlic, basil, olive oil, thyme, jalapeño (if desired), salt, and pepper in a bowl and let sit 2 hours or overnight. Combine mozzarella and ricotta cheeses. Cook pasta according to package directions, drain. Toss well with marinated tomatoes, then add the mozzarella mixture and toss again. Serve with Parmesan if desired.

Serves 4

Each Serving Provides:
821 calories, 22g protein, 43g fat, 91g carbohydrate,
16mg cholesterol, 10g dietary fiber, 364mg sodium

Noodles with Spicy Peanut Sauce

Preparation time: 20 minutes

This sauce, similar to many Asian dipping sauces, is best with fresh peanut butter. You might even check local health food stores where you can grind your own from peanuts. Make sure you use creamy, not chunky, peanut butter.

$1/3$ cup rice wine vinegar
$1/3$ cup tamari or soy sauce
$1/4$ cup water
3 teaspoons grated fresh ginger
1 clove garlic, minced
1 teaspoon sugar
7 tablespoons smooth peanut butter, room temperature
   or warmer
2 tablespoons peanut oil
5 tablespoons sesame oil
$1/4$ teaspoon hot pepper sauce
1 pound gemelli or other pasta
2 cups broccoli florets

Purée the vinegar, tamari, water, ginger, garlic, and sugar. Add peanut butter and blend again. With the blender running on low speed, add oils and blend well. Stir in hot pepper sauce. Steam broccoli 7 to 10 minutes. Cook pasta according to package directions, drain, toss with broccoli, and then with the sauce.

Serves 4

Each Serving Provides:
870 calories, 27g protein, 40g fat, 104g carbohydrate,
0mg cholesterol, 10g dietary fiber, 1502mg sodium

Main Dishes

*T*hese main dishes are for those who want to focus on what the vegetarian meal has, instead of what it's missing. When families enjoy many Italian, Chinese, and other ethnic dishes we certainly don't "miss the meat," and I don't think anyone cooking these main dishes will miss the meat either.

These recipes are family oriented, drawing on the ingredients I know my kids and their friends enjoy, and the foods adults and kids can enjoy together.

I hope your family will use many of these main dish recipes time and time again.

Rice & Vegetables with Coconut-Chile Sauce

Preparation time: 45 minutes

This sweet and spicy vegetable dish is a complete meal on its own. You may substitute a good-quality curry powder for the curry spices, if desired.

2 tablespoons extra-virgin olive oil
1 onion, finely chopped
2 cloves garlic, minced
2 teaspoons grated fresh ginger
$^1/_4$ teaspoon *each* cardamom, turmeric, coriander, cumin
$^1/_8$ teaspoon *each* ground cloves, mace
$^1/_2$ teaspoon sweet paprika
1 jalapeño, seeded and minced
$^1/_4$ cup coconut milk
1 tablespoon minced dried coconut
$1^1/_2$ cups water
2 cups vegetable broth or water
1 cup rice
2 zucchinis, sliced
1 small cauliflower, cut into pieces
2 tablespoons sour cream

Heat oil in a skillet and sauté onion until soft, about 5 minutes. Add garlic, ginger, spices, and jalapeño and cook another minute. Stir in coconut milk, dried coconut, and water; simmer 25 minutes, until thickened.

Meanwhile, heat broth or water to boiling and cook the rice, covered, 17 minutes, or until liquid is absorbed. Steam zucchini slices and cauliflower 6 minutes. Mix with rice. Stir sour cream into the onion mixture, pour sauce over the rice mixture, and serve.

Serves 4

Each Serving Provides:
385 calories, 11g protein, 13g fat, 60g carbohydrate,
3mg cholesterol, 8g dietary fiber, 31mg sodium

Vegetables Jambalaya

Preparation time: 30 minutes

Without the sausage or chicken this jambalaya offers a less earthy but fresher taste of Louisiana.

1 tablespoon oil
1 onion, chopped
1 bell pepper, seeded and chopped
5 cloves garlic, minced
2 green onions, chopped
2 tomatoes, chopped
1 teaspoon dried thyme
$1/8$ teaspoon ground cloves
$1/8$ teaspoon mace
1 bay leaf
$1/8$ teaspoon cayenne
$1/2$ teaspoon good-quality chili powder
2 cups vegetable broth
1 cup rice

Heat oil in a skillet and add onion and bell pepper. Sauté over medium heat 3 minutes, then add garlic, green onions, tomatoes, herbs, and spices. Stir together, add broth, and bring to a boil. Stir in the rice, cover, and simmer gently 20 minutes.

Serves 4

Each Serving Provides:
257 calories, 5g protein, 4g fat, 49g carbohydrate,
0mg cholesterol, 3g dietary fiber, 16mg sodium

Red Beans & Rice

Preparation time: 1 hour 50 minutes

This dish is traditionally made with meat. A little meat flavoring can be added into the broth if you're still trying to break the meat habit, and yearn for the flavor. If you are using fresh beans, soak first; see page 13.

2 cups cooked kidney beans or canned and drained
3 scallions, thinly sliced
2 cloves garlic, minced
$1/2$ onion, chopped
2 bay leaves
$1/8$ teaspoon red pepper flakes
$1/2$ teaspoon pepper
2 teaspoons salt
1 cup vegetable broth or water
$1/2$ cup tomato sauce (optional)
2 cups cooked rice

Mix everything except the rice in a large pot and cook, uncovered, over low heat for 60 minutes. Add rice and cook, covered, 30 minutes longer, or until sauce is thick and the beans are very tender.

Serves 4

Each Serving Provides:
305 calories, 14g protein, 1g fat, 61g carbohydrate,
0mg cholesterol, 6g dietary fiber, 1080mg sodium

Black & Red Bean Burritos

Preparation time: 30 minutes

Sautéed new potatoes go very nicely with the beans and spices in these filling burritos. Quick, and guaranteed to be enjoyed by the kids.

2 medium new potatoes
1 tablespoon olive oil
2 cloves garlic, minced
1 onion, chopped
$1/2$ jalapeño, seeded and minced
1 teaspoon ground cumin
1 teaspoon dried oregano
2 cups cooked black beans or canned, rinsed, and
    drained
1 cup cooked red kidney beans or canned and
    drained
$1/2$ cup vegetable broth or water
6 flour tortillas, warmed
1 tomato, sliced
$1/2$ cup chopped cilantro

Boil the potatoes until soft but not falling apart. Drain, cool slightly, and dice. Heat oil in a skillet and sauté the potatoes, garlic, onion, jalapeño, cumin, and oregano over low heat 8 minutes. Stir in the beans and broth. Cover and simmer 3 to 5 minutes, until warmed. Spoon the thick mixture into the tortillas, top with slices of tomato, sprinkle with cilantro.

Makes 6 burritos

Each Serving Provides:
342 calories, 15g protein, 5g fat, 61g carbohydrate,
0mg cholesterol, 9g dietary fiber, 70mg sodium

Chiles Rellenos
with Pineapple Salsa

Preparation time: 25 minutes

Choose lowfat cheese for this quick and delicious dish which already has less fat than the traditional egg batter rellenos.

4 poblano chiles
1 cup (4 ounces) grated jack cheese
1 cup (4 ounces) grated mozzarella cheese
2 cups pineapple rings
$1/2$ red bell pepper, seeded and diced
$1/2$ green bell pepper, seeded and diced
$1/2$ red onion, finely chopped
$1/4$ cup vegetable oil
2 tablespoons chopped fresh cilantro
1 tablespoon lime juice
1 tablespoon chopped fresh parsley
$1/2$ teaspoon red pepper flakes
Salsa (optional)

Roast chiles (see page 14), peel, slit along one side, and remove seeds. Combine cheeses and stuff into chiles. Preheat broiler. Place pineapple on a lightly oiled baking sheet. Broil each side until brown, about 5 minutes each. Remove from oven and cool. Dice pineapple and mix with remaining ingredients.

Place chiles on a baking sheet and broil until cheese melts. Serve with salsa.

Makes 4 rellenos

Each Serving Provides:
417 calories, 16g protein, 27g fat, 30g carbohydrate,
41mg cholesterol, 3g dietary fiber, 293mg sodium

Riso Primavera

Preparation time: 30 minutes

I like all-in-one meals. This is a sort of Pasta Primavera for rice and it is healthful, colorful eating.

2 tablespoons olive oil
2 tablespoons butter
1¹/₂ cups finely chopped onion
1¹/₂ cups rice
4¹/₂ cups vegetable broth or water
1 cup peas, fresh or defrosted
¹/₂ cup thinly sliced carrots
1 zucchini, cut into pieces
¹/₂ cup sliced green beans
¹/₄ cup chopped fresh parsley
1 clove garlic, minced
1 tablespoon lemon zest
1¹/₂ tablespoons lemon juice
2 tomatoes, diced with juice
¹/₄ teaspoon salt
¹/₈ teaspoon pepper
²/₃ cup grated Parmesan cheese

Heat oil and butter in a saucepan and sauté onions until soft, about 5 minutes. Add rice and stir to coat, about 3 minutes. Add broth and cook, covered, until absorbed, about 18 minutes. Meanwhile, blanch the peas, carrots, zucchini, and green beans or microwave until crisp-tender. Combine parsley, garlic, lemon zest, and lemon juice in a small bowl. Toss vegetables with rice, add parsley mixture, salt and pepper, and mix well. Top with Parmesan and serve.

Serves 4

Each Serving Provides:
540 calories, 16g protein, 18g fat, 79g carbohydrate, 27mg cholesterol, 5g dietary fiber, 509mg sodium

Sweet Herbed Zucchini

Preparation time: 35 minutes

These simple vegetables are something I prepare often.
The sweet thyme and dill flavors are soaked up by the
vegetables and the Parmesan on top is the perfect finish.
My kids always ask for more!

$^1/_4$ cup extra-virgin olive oil
1 sweet onion, cut in half and thinly sliced
2 cloves garlic, minced
3 zucchinis, sliced
4 to 5 mushrooms, sliced
2 tablespoons dried thyme
2 tablespoons dried dill
$^1/_4$ cup grated Parmesan cheese

Heat oil in a large skillet and add the onion, garlic, and
zucchini. Cook over low heat 10 minutes, then add mushrooms and herbs. Cook another 15 minutes or until vegetables are very soft. Remove to a lightly oiled baking
dish, cover with Parmesan, and broil until cheese melts,
about 2 minutes.

Serves 4

Each Serving Provides:
*221 calories, 7g protein, 16g fat, 16g carbohydrate,
4mg cholesterol, 5g dietary fiber, 107mg sodium*

Tamale Pie

Preparation time: 25 minutes (plus 40 minutes baking time)

A tamale pie always seems welcome. Use my chili recipe or your own in this pie.

4 cups Black & Red Bean Chili (page 32) or other
    vegetarian chili
1 cup tomato sauce
1 tomato, peeled and chopped, with juice
$^1/_2$ cup chopped olives
$^1/_8$ teaspoon seeded and minced jalapeño
$^3/_4$ cup yellow cornmeal
2 cups cold water
2 teaspoons olive or vegetable oil
1 cup grated cheddar or jack cheese

Preheat oven to 375°. Heat the chili, tomato sauce, tomato, olives, and jalapeño to simmer and cook 15 minutes.

Meanwhile, combine the cornmeal with the water until well blended. Bring to a boil then reduce heat and cook, stirring constantly, about 12 minutes or until thickened. Add the oil, mix well, then remove from heat.

Stir the cheese into the chili mixture, remove from heat. Pour the mixture into a lightly oiled baking dish and smooth, then cover with the cornmeal mixture. Bake 40 minutes.

Serves 5 to 6

Each Serving Provides:
346 calories, 18g protein, 13g fat, 39g carbohydrate,
18mg cholesterol, 13g dietary fiber, 610mg sodium

Tortilla Mole

Preparation time: 55 minutes

My teenager Andrew enjoyed a mole while visiting his
girlfriend's house for dinner. His enthusiasm encouraged
me to come up with my own version, and here it is.

2 tablespoons sesame or vegetable oil
2 onions, chopped
3 cloves garlic, minced
$^1/_4$ cup raisins
2 tablespoons seeded, peeled, and chopped chiles
   (see page 14 or use canned)
2 tomatoes, chopped
$^1/_4$ cup dry bread crumbs
$^1/_4$ cup prepared coffee
$^1/_8$ teaspoon cayenne
$^1/_4$ teaspoon cumin
$^1/_4$ teaspoon cinnamon
$^1/_8$ teaspoon anise
$^1/_4$ teaspoon allspice
1 tablespoon good-quality chili powder
$^1/_4$ teaspoon ground coriander
$1^1/_2$ cups vegetable broth or water
2 tablespoons grated unsweetened chocolate
4 cups grated jack or cheddar cheese
8 flour tortillas
Chopped fresh cilantro (optional)

Heat oil in a pot and gently sauté the onions and garlic until soft, about 7 minutes. Remove from pan and place in a processor or blender along with everything but the chocolate, tortillas, cheese, and cilantro. Process until smooth, then return to pot. Add 1¹/₂ cup broth and cook over medium-low heat 40 minutes, stirring often. Stir in the chocolate and cook 5 minutes more.

Divide cheese and spread over 4 tortillas. Top with remaining tortillas and place in a dry skillet or microwave and heat until cheese melts. Pour mole sauce over. Top with cilantro.

Serves 4

Each Serving Provides:
838 calories, 37g protein, 50g fat, 65g carbohydrate, 100mg cholesterol, 6g dietary fiber, 788mg sodium

Eggplant & Olive Stuffed Sweet Peppers

Preparation time: 20 minutes (plus 1 hour baking time)

I don't salt eggplant, although many cooks recommend it. Salting is done to remove extra moisture and bitterness. If desired, salt the eggplant in a colander and leave to drain for about an hour.

1 eggplant, diced
$^1/_4$ cup plus 2 tablespoons extra-virgin olive oil
$^2/_3$ cup pitted and sliced calamata olives
2 tomatoes, peeled, seeded, and chopped (fresh or canned)
2 cloves garlic, minced
$^1/_4$ teaspoon pepper
$^1/_4$ teaspoon dried oregano
2 tablespoons chopped fresh parsley
$^1/_3$ cup plain dry bread crumbs
4 red or green bell peppers, blanched, topped and seeded with membranes removed
$^1/_4$ cup crumbled feta cheese (optional)

Preheat oven to 350°. If you've salted the eggplant, rinse to wash off the salt and pat cubes dry. Heat $^1/_4$ cup olive oil in a skillet, add eggplant and cook, stirring occasionally, about 12 minutes, or until tender. Add olives, tomatoes, garlic, pepper, and oregano. Simmer 7 minutes.

Remove from heat, stir in the parsley and bread crumbs. Mix well, then stuff into bell peppers. Drizzle remaining 2 tablespoons oil over peppers. Place in a lightly oiled baking dish and bake 50 minutes. Remove, sprinkle feta cheese on top, and bake another 10 minutes.

Serves 4

Each Serving Provides:
338 calories, 4g protein, 28g fat, 23g carbohydrate, 0mg cholesterol, 3g dietary fiber, 669mg sodium

Rosemary Tart

Preparation time: 25 minutes (plus 20 minutes baking time)

Rosemary is a favorite for many cooks. I can't resist running my fingers over a rosemary bush or fresh rosemary leaves in the store. Here the flavor is put to good use in a pie.

$^1/_8$ cup minced fresh rosemary leaves or $1^1/_4$ tablespoons dried
1 bunch fresh spinach, stemmed, washed, dried, and
   chopped
$^1/_4$ cup feta cheese
1 clove garlic, minced
1 onion, chopped
$^1/_3$ cup milk
3 tablespoons oil plus additional for brushing dough
2 zucchinis, sliced
6 mushrooms, sliced
1 onion, halved and sliced
1 cup (1-inch pieces) broccoli florets
$^1/_2$ pound phyllo dough
3 red bell peppers, roasted and julienned (see page
   14 or use from jar)
2 cups chopped marinated artichoke hearts

Place the first six ingredients in a processor and purée. In a large skillet, heat about 1 tablespoon of oil and sauté the zucchini for 3 to 4 minutes, then remove and drain on paper towels. Repeat for mushrooms, onion, and broccoli. Preheat oven to 325°.

Line a deep pan with foil, with edges of foil rising above edge of pan, and rub with olive oil. Lay down 1 sheet phyllo and brush with oil. Repeat with remaining phyllo.

Pour the purée over phyllo and then add zucchini, mushrooms, onion, broccoli, peppers, and artichokes on top. Bake 20 minutes, until crust is golden.

Serves 6

Each Serving Provides:
409 calories, 10g protein, 22g fat, 49g carbohydrate,
5mg cholesterol, 8g dietary fiber, 608mg sodium

Vegetarian Paella

Preparation time: 1 hour

This is my version of the hearty Spanish classic. This dish is a little different, with a hint of fresh ginger to go with many traditional ingredients.

2 tablespoons extra-virgin olive oil
2 onions, chopped
3 cloves garlic, minced
1 can (28 ounces) tomatoes
2 bell peppers, red or green, seeded and julienned
4 artichoke hearts, sliced
2 cups peas, fresh or frozen
5 cups vegetable broth or water
1 teaspoon grated fresh ginger
$1/2$ teaspoon paprika
$1/4$ teaspoon salt
$1^3/4$ cups arborio rice
$1/4$ teaspoon pepper

In a large skillet, heat oil and sauté the onions and garlic until soft, about 6 minutes. Add the tomatoes and cook, breaking up in pan, another 5 minutes. Add bell peppers, artichoke hearts, and peas along with $2^1/2$ cups broth and simmer, covered, for 10 minutes. Stir in the ginger, paprika, and salt. Stir in the rice and remaining $2^{1}/_{2}$ cups broth and bring to a boil. Reduce heat and simmer, covered, stirring occasionally, 20 minutes or until liquid is absorbed. Top with pepper.

Serves 4

Each Serving Provides:
565 calories, 14g protein, 9g fat, 109g carbohydrate,
0mg cholesterol, 7g dietary fiber, 568mg sodium

Asparagus-Shallot Risotto

Preparation time: 30 minutes

The fresh taste of asparagus mixed with shallots gives this
creamy rice dish a wonderful flavor. I like to serve it with
a cup of minestrone soup and bread.

7 cups vegetable broth or water
1 tablespoon extra-virgin olive oil
3 shallots, peeled and sliced
1 onion, diced
1 clove garlic, minced
1³/4 cups arborio rice
¹/8 teaspoon pepper
1 cup (1-inch pieces) asparagus
8 crimini or button mushrooms, sliced
3 to 4 tablespoons chopped fresh basil
Grated Parmesan cheese (optional)

Place broth or water in a pot and begin to heat.
Meanwhile, heat oil and sauté shallots, onion, and garlic
about 4 minutes, then add rice and pepper and stir
another 5 minutes.

When the broth boils, remove from heat then add
rice mixture. Return to heat and simmer 14 minutes, stirring frequently.

Toss asparagus and mushrooms, then steam or microwave (see page 2). Add them, along with the basil, to the rice and cook another 3 to 4 minutes, until creamy. Add Parmesan cheese if desired.

Serves 4

Each Serving Provides:
432 calories, 11g protein, 5g fat, 87g carbohydrate,
0mg cholesterol, 3g dietary fiber, 27mg sodium

Cilantro Cheese Stuffed Peppers

Preparation time: 30 minutes (plus 20 minutes baking time)

This is best with poblanos, but does well with Anaheim peppers as well. See page 14 for tips on roasted and peeling chile peppers.

$^1/_2$ cup Mexican white or jack cheese, grated
$^1/_2$ cup grated feta cheese
$^1/_2$ cup plus 1 tablespoon minced fresh cilantro
$^1/_2$ teaspoon oregano
8 poblano chiles, roasted, peeled, and seeded, tops
  removed
2 tablespoons olive oil
$^1/_2$ onion, chopped
2 cloves garlic, minced
3 tomatoes, peeled, with juice (see page 14) or 1 can
  (16 ounces)
$^1/_2$ teaspoon dried thyme

Preheat oven to 350°. Combine cheeses, $^1/_2$ cup cilantro, and oregano in a bowl. Fill the peppers with the mixture and place in an oiled baking dish that fits all.
     Pour oil in a skillet and mix in the onion and garlic. Heat and sauté until soft, about 8 minutes. Add the tomatoes and thyme and cook down, about 20 minutes. Remove to a blender and purée. Pour over peppers and bake 20 minutes. Top with remaining 1 tablespoon cilantro.

Makes 8 stuffed peppers

Each Serving Provides:
115 calories, 5g protein, 7g fat, 9g carbohydrate,
13mg cholesterol, 2g dietary fiber, 130mg sodium

Mozzarella Potato Pancakes

Preparation time: 35 minutes

Potatoes mixed with cheese and peppers makes a cozy
dinner. Serve with a vegetable salad.

3 to 4 baking potatoes, about 2 pounds
$^1/_4$ cup minced sweet onion
$^1/_4$ cup minced bell pepper, green, red, or yellow
$^1/_4$ teaspoon salt
$^1/_4$ teaspoon pepper
1 egg, lightly beaten
2 tablespoons heavy cream
$^3/_4$ cup grated mozzarella cheese
2 tablespoons vegetable oil

Boil the unpeeled potatoes about 15 to 20 minutes until
not quite cooked. Cool and peel, then grate with a hand
grater or food processor. Mix potatoes together with the
onion, bell pepper, salt, and pepper. Combine egg and
cream well, then mix into potato mixture. Add cheese.
Form into cakes. Heat oil in a skillet or griddle and cook
about 4 minutes on each side over medium heat.

Serves 4 to 6

Each Serving Provides:
220 calories, 7g protein, 10g fat, 27g carbohydrate,
51mg cholesterol, 1g dietary fiber, 176mg sodium

Zucchini Stuffed with Corn, Carrots, & Cheese

Preparation time: 20 minutes (plus 25 minutes baking time)

When there are just too many zucchinis and plenty of fresh corn, this dish is welcome and fast. Try it with a pasta salad on the side.

6 zucchinis, halved lengthwise
2 tablespoons vegetable or olive oil
1 carrot, thinly sliced and minced
$^1/_2$ sweet onion, minced
3 cloves garlic, minced
3 cups corn kernels, fresh (cut from 6 ears) or
   defrosted
$^1/_8$ teaspoon red pepper flakes
2 tablespoons chopped parsley
1 tablespoon chopped fresh oregano or 1 teaspoon
   dried
$^3/_4$ cup grated jack cheese

Preheat oven to 375°. Scoop out the zucchini and reserve. Spread 1 tablespoon oil on the zucchini and place on a baking sheet cut side down. Bake 15 minutes. Meanwhile, heat remaining 1 tablespoon oil and sauté the carrot and onion until soft, about 5 minutes. Add garlic, corn, and red pepper flakes and sauté another 7 to 8 minutes. Add 1 cup of zucchini pulp and sauté until warm, 1 to 2 minutes. Remove from heat and mix in the parsley and oregano. Generously stuff the mixture into zucchini, place in an oiled baking dish, cover with foil, and bake 25 minutes. Remove from oven, sprinkle with cheese, and return to oven until cheese is melted.

Serves 4 to 6

Each Serving Provides:
214 calories, 9g protein, 10g fat, 27g carbohydrate, 13mg cholesterol, 6g dietary fiber, 93mg sodium

Flavorful Fried Rice

Preparation time: 25 minutes

Cold rice works best when making any fried rice. This combination goes surprisingly well with fruit.

$^1/_2$ cup green bean pieces
3 tablespoons vegetable oil
1 onion, chopped
$^1/_2$ jalapeño, seeded and minced
1 clove garlic, minced
1 red pepper, seeded and finely chopped
1 stalk celery, sliced
1 teaspoon minced fresh thyme or $^1/_2$ teaspoon dried
2 tablespoons tomato sauce
$^1/_2$ cup pineapple chunks (optional)
4 cups cooked rice

Steam or microwave the green beans until crisp tender, see page 5. Set aside. Heat oil and sauté the onion, jalapeño, garlic, red pepper, and celery until onions are soft, about 8 minutes. Add the thyme, tomato sauce, and cooked beans; cook another 5 minutes. Stir in pineapple and rice, breaking up to mix well and heat through.

Serves 4 to 6

Each Serving Provides:
266 calories, 5g protein, 8g fat, 44g carbohydrate,
0mg cholesterol, 2g dietary fiber, 24mg sodium

Vegetables with Tarator

Preparation time: 20 minutes

This Middle Eastern dish is slightly different in each country, primarily because a different nut is used. The sauce should have the consistency of yogurt.

1 small cauliflower, cut into pieces
2 zucchinis, sliced
2 bell peppers, red or green, seeded and diced
1 small eggplant, diced
1/2 cup green beans, trimmed and cut into pieces
1 cup pine nuts, walnuts, or hazelnuts
2 cloves garlic, minced
4 tablespoons tahini
3 tablespoons red wine vinegar
1/8 teaspoon cayenne
2 tablespoons olive oil or vegetable broth

Steam vegetables until crisp tender then mix together in a bowl. Process remaining ingredients, except oil, in a blender, remove to a bowl and stir in the oil or broth to desired consistency. Serve over or with cooked vegetables.

Serves 4 to 6

Each Serving Provides:
187 calories, 7g protein, 11g fat, 19g carbohydrate,
0mg cholesterol, 7g dietary fiber, 25mg sodium

Corn & Black Bean Tostadas

Preparation time: 25 minutes

This is one of my favorite meals for rushed nights. If you like, spread some fresh spinach leaves on the tortillas before adding the black bean mixture.

2 cups canned black beans, rinsed and drained
$3/4$ teaspoon salt
1 jalapeño, seeded and minced
1 cup fresh corn (cut from 2 ears), or defrosted
1 sweet onion, diced
2 tablespoons lime juice
3 cloves garlic, minced
$1/2$ teaspoon cumin
$1/8$ teaspoon cayenne
1 large tomato, peeled, seeded, and coarsely chopped
1 cup loosely packed, chopped cilantro
Oil for frying
6 flour tortillas
Jack cheese (optional)
Sour cream (optional)

Place beans in a saucepan and heat. Add the salt, jalapeño, corn, and onion and warm over low heat 10 minutes. Add remaining ingredients, except oil, tortillas, and optional items, and mix well. Remove from heat.

In a skillet over medium heat, heat enough vegetable oil to immerse one tortilla. Add tortillas, one at a time, to hot oil and cook on each side until crisp, about 2 minutes. Drain on paper towels and top with black bean mixture. Top with cheese or sour cream if desired.

Makes 6 tostadas

Each Serving Provides:
219 calories, 9g protein, 2g fat, 42g carbohydrate, 0mg cholesterol, 3g dietary fiber, 636mg sodium

Vegetarian Potpie

Preparation time: 45 minutes (plus time to make dough)

Who says potpies must have chicken or beef? This flavorful vegetarian pie is a favorite of ours.

1 pie shell (see page 11)
2 tablespoons extra-virgin olive oil
1 onion, chopped
$^1/_2$ eggplant, diced
1 bell pepper, seeded and diced
4 mushrooms, sliced
3 tablespoons flour
$^1/_2$ cup peas, fresh or frozen
$^1/_2$ cup corn kernels, fresh (cut from 1 ear) or frozen
$1^1/_2$ cups vegetable broth or water
$^1/_2$ teaspoon dried oregano
$^1/_2$ teaspoon dried thyme
$^1/_2$ teaspoon dried rosemary
$^1/_4$ teaspoon salt
$^1/_4$ teaspoon pepper

Preheat oven to 400°. Heat oil and sauté the onion, eggplant, bell pepper, and mushrooms until soft, about 8 minutes. Add flour and mix well, then stir in the remaining ingredients and remove from heat. Place the pie crust in a lightly oiled baking dish and spoon vegetable mixture into the pie. Cover with top crust. Prick with a fork to vent. Bake 25 minutes.

Serves 4 to 6

Each Serving Provides:
234 calories, 5g protein, 10g fat, 32g carbohydrate,
14mg cholesterol, 3g dietary fiber, 151mg sodium

Ratatouille Pie

Preparation time: 40 minutes (plus time to make dough and 55 minutes baking time)

My family enjoys many ratatouille dishes, from pizza to shortened versions of the original. This potpie is filling and delicious.

1 pie shell (see page 11)
1 tablespoon extra-virgin olive oil
$^1/_2$ onion, diced
1 clove garlic, minced
$^1/_2$ zucchini, sliced (about 1 cup)
1 small eggplant, peeled and diced (about 2 cups)
$^1/_2$ bell pepper, red or green, seeded and diced
2 teaspoons minced fresh basil or 1 teaspoon dried
1 teaspoon dried oregano
$^1/_2$ teaspoon dried thyme
1 tomato, peeled and diced
1 cup (4 ounces) grated mozzarella
3 eggs, beaten
$^1/_3$ cup milk

Heat oil in skillet and sauté the onion and garlic 3 to 4 minutes over low heat, then add zucchini, eggplant, bell pepper, basil, oregano, and thyme. Sauté over low heat

15 to 20 minutes, until soft. Remove from heat and combine with the tomato and mozzarella. Place the pastry into a lightly oiled baking dish. Spoon vegetable mixture into the pastry. Combine the eggs and milk well, then pour over vegetables. Bake 50 minutes or until set. Let stand 5 minutes before serving.

Serves 4 to 6

Each Serving Provides:
266 calories, 12g protein, 14g fat, 24g carbohydrate,
132mg cholesterol, 2g dietary fiber, 177mg sodium

Leek, Sweet Pepper, & Potato Cakes

Preparation time: 30 minutes

If you are in a hurry you can use the grated, refrigerated potatoes from the grocery store (although it can be hard to find just plain grated potatoes; many have spices and other things added). Be careful to wash the leek thoroughly. These cakes are great with a vegetable salad or a soup.

2 pounds potatoes, peeled
5 tablespoons olive oil
1 red bell pepper, seeded and finely chopped
1 leek, including green top, chopped
$1/2$ teaspoon salt
$1/2$ teaspoon pepper
$1/4$ pound (1 cup) fontina or Gruyère cheese, sliced
    (optional)
Sour cream or salsa (optional)

Cover potatoes with water and let stand 2 to 3 minutes. Change water and let stand another couple of minutes, then drain. Shred the potatoes, place in a towel, and wring to remove excess moisture. Place in a mixing bowl.

Heat 2 tablespoons of oil in a skillet and sauté pepper 3 to 4 minutes, then add leeks and sauté another 4 to 5 minutes, until soft. Remove and mix well with the potatoes, salt, and pepper.

Heat remaining 3 tablespoons oil, add all of the potato mixture (or add $^1/_3$ cup at a time for individual cakes) and flatten with a spatula. Cover and cook over medium heat 5 to 6 minutes, until browned. Turn and cook on the other side until browned, 4 to 5 minutes. If desired, place slices of cheese over cooked cake and place under a broiler 1 to 2 minutes to melt. Or serve with sour cream or salsa.

Serves 4

Each Serving Provides:
336 calories, 4g protein, 17g fat, 44g carbohydrate,
0mg cholesterol, 4g dietary fiber, 279mg sodium

Sweet Pepper & Rosemary Pie

Preparation time: 35 minutes (plus time to make dough and 35 minutes baking time)

I tend to make this pie during the summer when peppers are at their best, and so is my rosemary bush.

4 tablespoons extra-virgin olive oil
1 *each* red, yellow, and green bell peppers, seeded and thinly sliced
1 sweet onion, halved and thinly sliced
2 cloves garlic, minced
$1/3$ cup water
15 calamata olives, pitted and sliced
$1/4$ cup fresh minced rosemary leaves
$1/4$ cup grated Parmesan cheese
2 eggs plus 2 egg yolks
$1^1/2$ cups heavy cream
Pie shell (see page 11)
1 cup grated mozzarella

Preheat oven to 400°. Place 2 tablespoons of olive oil in a skillet, add the bell peppers and onion. Coat, then sauté over medium heat 5 minutes. Add garlic, sauté another 3 minutes, add water and cover. Cook until peppers and onion are very soft, about 15 minutes. Remove from heat and stir in the olives.

In a small skillet, warm remaining 2 tablespoons oil over low heat and add the rosemary. Warm until aromatic, about 3 minutes, then remove from heat, cool and combine with Parmesan. Set aside.

Beat the eggs and yolks together, then add cream. Place the pie crust in a lightly oiled baking dish. Brush with rosemary paste then spread ¹/₂ cup mozzarella followed by the pepper mixture. Add remaining ¹/₂ cup mozzarella and the egg mixture. Bake 35 minutes, or until set.

Serves 4 to 6

Each Serving Provides:
465 calories, 14g protein, 34g fat, 28g carbohydrate, 137mg cholesterol, 2g dietary fiber, 396mg sodium

Enchiladas Verdes

Preparation time: 50 minutes (plus 20 minutes baking time)

Serve this dish with rice and beans, if desired, for a complete Mexican dinner.

FOR THE SAUCE:
1 pound (about 11) fresh tomatillos, husked and
   washed, or 2 cans (13 ounces *each*)
Fresh green chiles: 2 serranos, 1 jalapeño or for a
   mild sauce, 2 Anaheim peppers
5 sprigs fresh cilantro
1 small onion, chopped
1 clove garlic, chopped or minced
5 fresh basil leaves, chopped (optional)
6 to 7 fresh mint leaves, chopped (optional)
1 tablespoon vegetable oil
2 cups broth
Salt

FOR THE ENCHILADAS:
1 tablespoon vegetable oil
$1/2$ sweet onion, diced
1 jalapeño, seeded and minced
1 bell pepper, seeded and sliced
1 teaspoon ground cumin
$1/8$ teaspoon salt
3 cloves garlic, minced
2 cups corn, fresh (cut from 2 ears) or frozen
Oil for frying
12 corn tortillas
2 cups shredded jack or cheddar cheese
4 tablespoons chopped cilantro

FOR THE SAUCE: Boil the tomatillos and chiles in salted water until just tender, about 10 minutes. (If using canned tomatillos, simply drain.) Drain tomatillo mixture, seed the chiles, and place in a blender or processor with the cilantro, onion, garlic, basil, and mint and blend until smooth. Heat the oil in a skillet over medium-high heat. Pour the sauce in and stir 5 minutes. Add broth, return to a boil, and reduce heat to medium. Simmer until thick, about 10 minutes. Salt to taste.

Makes about 3 cups

FOR THE FILLING: Preheat oven to 350°. Heat 1 tablespoon oil in a skillet and sauté onion about 5 minutes. Add the peppers, cumin, salt, garlic, and corn and sauté another 5 minutes, until corn is just cooked. Remove from heat.

Heat the oil in a skillet and dip the tortillas in, one at a time, to just heat, about 5 seconds. Use paper towels to absorb the excess oil. Dip the tortillas in the sauce, then place in an oiled baking dish. Spoon a little of the filling into the tortilla then top with cheese and cilantro. Roll the tortilla up against the wall of the dish and repeat until all tortillas are filled. Pour 1 to 2 cups of sauce over the tortillas then top with any extra (or additional) cheese, if desired. Bake 20 minutes, until sauce is bubbling.

Serves 4 to 6

Each Serving Provides:
392 calories, 15g protein, 17g fat, 47g carbohydrate,
33mg cholesterol, 6g dietary fiber, 362mg sodium

Zucchini Tetrazzini

Preparation time: 30 minutes (plus 20 minutes baking time)

Turkey tetrazzini was a favorite of ours, with its rich flavors of spices and butter. Here is a recipe that is lower in fat, better for your health, and, I think, just as delicious.

8 ounces spaghettini or other thin pasta
3 zucchinis, julienned
2 tablespoons vegetable oil or butter
$1/2$ onion, diced
2 cloves garlic, minced
$1/4$ teaspoon dried basil
2 scallions, minced
3 to 4 mushrooms, sliced
2 tablespoons butter
2 tablespoons flour
$1/4$ cup milk
$1/4$ cup plain yogurt
1 teaspoon lemon juice
$1/4$ cup chopped fresh parsley
$1/4$ cup vegetable broth or water
$1/4$ teaspoon pepper
$1/2$ cup grated Parmesan cheese

Preheat oven to 375°. Cook pasta according to package directions, drain. Steam zucchini for 5 minutes, to soften slightly. In a skillet, heat oil over low heat and add the onion, garlic, and basil. Sauté 3 minutes, add the scallions, sauté another 3 minutes. Add mushrooms and sauté another 3 to 4 minutes.

Heat butter in a saucepan over medium-low heat and stir in the flour. Stir constantly for 2 minutes. Reduce heat to low, stir in milk, yogurt ($1/2$ cup heavy cream may be substituted for milk and yogurt), lemon juice, parsley, broth, and pepper and cook 3 to 4 minutes, until thick. Add mushroom mixture, cooked zucchini, and pasta and mix well. Place in a lightly oiled baking dish, sprinkle with cheese, and bake until bubbly, about 20 minutes.

Serves 4

Each Serving Provides:
466 calories, 17g protein, 18g fat, 60g carbohydrate,
26mg cholesterol, 6g dietary fiber, 277mg sodium

Empanadas with Romesco Sauce

Preparation time: 90 minutes

There are as many different types of empanadas as there are South American cities, it seems. Most versions have meat, and many are deep-fried. These vegetarian versions are baked.

FOR THE DOUGH:
3 cups flour
1 teaspoon salt
4 tablespoons butter, cut into small pieces
6 tablespoons olive oil
6 to 8 tablespoons cold water

FOR THE FILLING:
1 tablespoon oil
1 onion, diced
2 zucchinis, diced
2 tomatoes, chopped
4 to 5 mushrooms, sliced
1 tablespoon ground coriander
2 teaspoons cumin
$^1/_4$ teaspoon cayenne
2 red bell peppers, roasted, seeded, and diced (see page 14)
2 new potatoes, boiled until soft and diced
4 tablespoons chopped fresh cilantro
2 eggs, lightly beaten

FOR THE SAUCE:
1 tomato, peeled, seeded and chopped
$^1/_2$ bell pepper, seeded and chopped

1 tablespoon seeded and chopped jalapeño,
  or 2 teaspoons red pepper flakes
2 cloves garlic, minced
2 tablespoons almonds, toasted
$^3/_4$ cup olive oil
$^1/_3$ cup dry white wine or vegetable broth
$^1/_8$ teaspoon salt
$^1/_8$ teaspoon pepper

FOR THE DOUGH: Sift the flour and salt into a bowl. Mix
in the butter, then the oil, mixing well. Add water a little
at a time, mixing well, until smooth. Cover and refrigerate
for 1 hour.

FOR THE FILLING: Heat oil in a skillet and sauté the
onion until soft, about 6 minutes. Add zucchini, tomatoes,
mushrooms, and spices and continue to cook until softened, about 7 to 10 minutes. Add the roasted peppers and
potatoes and stir for a minute or two. Remove from heat
and stir in the cilantro.

Preheat oven to 350°. Divide the dough into nine
pieces and roll into balls. Flatten into 5-inch circles and
place 1 or 2 tablespoons of the filling mixture in the center. Brush the edge of the dough circle with a little water,
then fold over into a half moon, crimping the edges
together with a fork. Brush each empanada with a little
beaten egg. Place on a greased baking sheet and bake 30
minutes or until crust is brown.

FOR THE SAUCE: Combine the tomato, bell pepper,
jalapeño, garlic, almonds, oil, wine or broth, salt, and pepper in a blender and purée. Pour sauce over empanadas
and serve hot or at room temperature.

Makes 9 empanadas

Each Serving Provides:
*538 calories, 9g protein, 35g fat, 47g carbohydrate,
62mg cholesterol, 4g dietary fiber, 348mg sodium*

Spinach & Potato Casserole

Preparation time: 30 minutes (plus 50 minutes baking time)

This is especially good if your diet will allow you the extra cheese. Nice on its own, or serve with a soup or green salad.

6 to 7 red potatoes (about 3 pounds), peeled and cut
   into pieces of equal size
1 cup milk at room temperature
5 cups packed fresh spinach or 1 package
   (10 ounces) frozen
2 tablespoons oil or butter
1 onion, diced
$1/3$ cup grated Parmesan cheese
$1/2$ teaspoon pepper
$1/2$ teaspoon salt
$1/2$ cup grated Gruyère or fontina cheese(optional)

Preheat oven to 375°. Boil potatoes until tender, 20 to 25 minutes. Remove to a bowl with a slotted spoon and mash. Stir in the milk, adding a little more if necessary, until creamy and moist. Set aside. Clean spinach leaves and drain, but do not dry. Steam 4 minutes, until wilted. (If using frozen spinach cook according to package directions.) Squeeze excess liquid from spinach and set aside.

    Place oil or butter in a skillet and sauté the onion until soft, about 6 minutes. Remove from heat and stir in the spinach and Parmesan cheese. Add this to potatoes along with the spices and combine well. Lightly oil a baking dish and pour potato mixture in and spread with cheese, if desired, on top. Cover and bake 25 minutes. Uncover and bake another 25 minutes.

Serves 4 to 6

Each Serving Provides:
303 calories, 9g protein, 7g fat, 53g carbohydrate,
7mg cholesterol, 5g dietary fiber, 329mg sodium

Corn Tamales with Green Sauce

Preparation time: 1 hour (plus 1¹/₂ hours cooking time)

These take a little while to make but the results are wonderful. They keep in the refrigerator for a few days too, sealed in a plastic bag.

9 ears corn (about 4 cups kernels)
¹/₂ cup (1 stick) butter, softened
¹/₂ cup cubed jack cheese
1 cup masa harina (flour for making tortillas, available in many stores)
4 fresh Anaheim chiles, peeled, seeded, and chopped, or 1 can (12 ounces) small green chiles, chopped
1 pound (about 11) fresh tomatillos, husked and washed, or 2 cans (13 ounces *each*)
2 to 3 fresh jalapeños, seeded
5 sprigs cilantro, coarsely chopped
1 small onion, chopped
1 clove garlic, chopped or minced
6 to 7 fresh mint leaves, chopped (optional)
2 tablespoons vegetable oil
2 cups vegetable broth
¹/₄ teaspoon salt

Remove outer shucks from the corn, then carefully remove inner shucks, keeping them whole. Trim pointed end and drop the shucks in hot, but not boiling water. Turn off the heat and let sit while you cut the kernels off the corn. In a blender or food processor combine the butter, cheese, masa, and a little hot water from the husks and blend until smooth. Stir in chiles and set aside.

Boil the tomatillos and jalapeños in salted water until just tender, about 10 minutes, then drain. (If using canned tomatillos simply drain). Place in a blender or food processor with the cilantro, onion, garlic, and mint and blend until smooth. Heat the oil in a skillet over medium-high heat. Pour sauce in and stir for 5 minutes. Add broth and salt, return to boil then simmer 8 to 10 minutes, until thickened.

To make the tamales, spread a husk and place 2 to 3 tablespoons of corn filling in the center, fold the sides over the filling and fold ends up. Stand tamales in a colander or steamer in a pot large enough to hold all. Bring water to a boil and steam, with the tamales above the water, for 90 minutes, adding more water as needed. Serve with the green sauce.

Makes about 20 tamales

Each Serving Provides:
130 calories, 3g protein, 8g fat, 14g carbohydrate,
16mg cholesterol, 2g dietary fiber, 95mg sodium

Creole Vegetables

Preparation time: 25 minutes

This nicely tangy vegetable dish reflects the flavors of Cajun country. It's a complete meal all by itself, or serve with soup or bread.

1 cup rice
2 1/2 cups water or vegetable broth
3 bell peppers, red, yellow, and green
4 tablespoons olive oil
4 mushrooms, sliced
2 zucchinis, sliced
1/2 onion, finely chopped
1 stalk celery, finely chopped
2 cloves garlic, minced
1/4 teaspoon sweet paprika
1/2 teaspoon ground coriander
1/8 teaspoon cayenne
1/8 teaspoon chili powder
1/2 teaspoon dried basil
1/2 teaspoon dried thyme
1/2 teaspoon pepper
1/2 cup vegetable broth
1/2 cup tomato sauce
Hot pepper sauce to taste

Cook rice or broth, covered, for 17 minutes. Seed and julienne all but half of a bell pepper. Heat 2 tablespoons oil and sauté the julienned peppers with the mushrooms and zucchini until crisp tender, about 6 minutes.

Finely chop remaining half bell pepper. Heat remaining 2 tablespoons oil in a large skillet. Stir in the onion, finely chopped peppers, celery, and garlic. Add seasonings and mix well. Sauté over low heat, stirring occasionally, until onion and peppers are soft, about 8 minutes. Add remaining ingredients, increase heat to a boil, then simmer uncovered until sauce thickens, about 15 minutes. Mix rice and vegetables then pour sauce on top.

Serves 4

Each Serving Provides:
358 calories, 7g protein, 15g fat, 52g carbohydrate,
0mg cholesterol, 5g dietary fiber, 116mg sodium

Spicy Black Beans & Yellow Rice

Preparation time: 40 minutes

Black beans are among the most versatile foods. Here they are paired with spiced rice to make a great side dish or entrée.

3 tablespoons olive oil
4 cloves garlic, minced
1 onion, chopped
$1/2$ red or green bell pepper, seeded and diced
1 small jalapeño, seeded and minced
3 cups cooked black beans or canned and drained
1 teaspoon good-quality chili powder
$1/2$ teaspoon ground cumin
$2^1/2$ cups vegetable broth or water
1 cup rice
$1/2$ teaspoon ground turmeric
$1/2$ teaspoon grated fresh ginger
$1/4$ teaspoon ground coriander
Grated Parmesan cheese (optional)

Heat 2 tablespoons of oil in a pot and add 3 garlic cloves, the onion and peppers and sauté over low heat, about 12 minutes. Add the beans, chili powder, cumin, and $1/2$ cup of broth or water and cook, uncovered, 30 minutes, until the beans are hot.

In a saucepan heat remaining tablespoon of oil and sauté remaining garlic clove about 3 minutes. Add remaining 2 cups of broth or water, bring to a boil, then stir in the rice, reduce heat and cook, covered, 17 minutes. Stir remaining spices into the rice, then mix the cooked rice with the bean mixture. Top with grated cheese if desired.

Serves 4

Each Serving Provides:
804 calories, 37g protein, 13g fat, 139g carbohydrate,
0mg cholesterol, 22g dietary fiber, 22mg sodium

Samosa Sauté

Preparation time: 45 minutes

This is a filling for samosas, the deep-fried Indian dish.
This mixture can be stuffed into a calzone and baked, or
enjoyed as is. I just happen to like it as a sauté rather than
packed in a pie.

6 potatoes, peeled and quartered
2 tablespoons oil
1 onion, chopped
1 tablespoon grated fresh ginger
1 teaspoon *each* cardamom, turmeric, coriander,
  cumin
$^1/_2$ teaspoon *each* ground cloves, mace, fenugreek
$^1/_4$ teaspoon cayenne
2 teaspoons sweet paprika
3 tomatoes, sliced
2 cups trimmed and sliced green beans
1 tablespoon lemon juice
1 teaspoon lemon zest

Boil the potatoes until tender, but not falling apart. Heat
the oil in a skillet and sauté the onion until soft. Add ginger and curry spices (or substitute 2 tablespoons good-
quality curry powder for all but the ginger) and sauté
another 2 to 3 minutes. Stir in the tomatoes and green

beans and cook another 15 minutes over low heat. Add the potatoes and cook another 4 or 5 minutes, then stir in the lemon juice and lemon zest.

Serves 4

Rice with Vegetables & Curry

Preparation time: 25 minutes

This rich dish is filled with wonderful flavors cooked into
the rice and vegetables. Adjust the spice as desired, with
more or less cayenne. A complete dinner on its own.

3 tablespoons oil
1 onion, chopped
2 tablespoons grated fresh ginger
2 cloves garlic, minced
1 teaspoon *each* cardamom, turmeric, coriander,
   cumin
$^1/_2$ teaspoon cayenne
$^1/_8$ teaspoon ground cloves
2 teaspoons sweet paprika
$^1/_2$ teaspoon salt
$^1/_2$ teaspoon pepper
1 cup rice
2 carrots, sliced
$1^1/_2$ cups trimmed and sliced green beans
1 cup coarsely chopped cauliflower florets
2 cups peeled and diced Yukon gold or new potatoes
2 cups vegetable broth or water
$^1/_3$ cup finely chopped flaked coconut
$^1/_4$ cup plain yogurt
$^1/_4$ cup milk
$^1/_2$ cup chopped roasted cashews

Heat oil in a large skillet and sauté the onion, ginger, and garlic over low heat for 10 minutes. Add the curry spices (or substitute 2 tablespoons good-quality curry powder), salt, and pepper and stir until aromatic, 1 or 2 minutes. Stir in the rice and stir constantly until golden, 3 to 4 minutes. Add vegetables, stir to mix, add broth or water. Bring to a boil, cover, reduce heat and cook 18 minutes, or until liquid is absorbed.

Combine coconut, yogurt, and milk and pour over vegetables. Sprinkle with cashews and serve.

Serves 4 to 6

Each Serving Provides:
368 calories, 8g protein, 16g fat, 51g carbohydrate,
1mg cholesterol, 4g dietary fiber, 213mg sodium

Muenster Quesadillas

Preparation time: 15 minutes

This quick dinner has a fresh taste and looks great on the plate. Perfect with rice, to which a tablespoon or two of fresh chopped cilantro has been added after cooking.

8 flour tortillas
2 cups (8 ounces) grated Muenster cheese
2 tomatoes, thinly sliced
1 red bell pepper, seeded, roasted, peeled, and
    chopped (see page 14)
^{1}/2 cup chopped fresh cilantro
1 tablespoon vegetable or olive oil
1 tablespoon butter, melted
1 cucumber, thinly sliced
Salsa or sour cream (optional)

Sprinkle ^{1}/2 cup of the cheese onto one of the tortillas, then place ^{1}/4 of the tomatoes and red peppers on top. Sprinkle with 2 tablespoons cilantro, then cover with another tortilla. Combine oil and butter and brush outside of both tortillas. Repeat with remaining tortillas. Grill or fry until golden and cheese has melted. Garnish with sliced cucumber and serve with salsa or sour cream, if desired.

Makes 4 quesadillas

Each Serving Provides:
*482 calories, 18g protein, 28g fat, 41g carbohydrate,
62mg cholesterol, 3g dietary fiber, 508mg sodium*

Vegetarian Goulash Casserole

Preparation time: 20 minutes (plus 35 minutes baking time)

My kids always loved my meat goulash and we enjoy the same flavors without the meat in this healthful vegetarian version. While this cooks you can throw together a salad.

1 pound egg noodles
1 tablespoon oil
1 onion, chopped
1/2 bell pepper, seeded and diced
1 1/2 cups plain yogurt
1/2 cup cottage cheese
1 cup sour cream
1 teaspoon paprika
1/2 cup tomato juice
3/4 cup Parmesan cheese

Preheat oven to 350°. Cook noodles according to package directions, drain. Heat oil in a skillet and sauté the onion and bell pepper until soft, about 6 minutes. In a lightly oiled baking dish mix the noodles with all ingredients except the cheese. Bake 30 minutes, top with cheese, and bake another 5 minutes.

Serves 4

Each Serving Provides:
738 calories, 33g protein, 24g fat, 98g carbohydrate,
160mg cholesterol, 4g dietary fiber, 470mg sodium

Vegie Stir-Fry with Rice Noodles

Preparation time: 25 minutes

This dish is fast, and so colorful you'll want to serve it for guests.

1 pound rice noodles
2 tablespoons tamari or soy sauce
1 teaspoon cornstarch
1 tablespoon grated fresh ginger
3 tablespoons white wine
$^{1}/_{2}$ teaspoon sesame oil
1 red bell pepper, seeded and julienned
4 mushrooms, sliced
1 cup snow peas
$^{1}/_{3}$ cup vegetable broth or water, heated

Cook noodles according to package directions, drain. Combine 1 tablespoon tamari with cornstarch and ginger. Place remaining tablespoon of tamari in a wok or skillet with wine and sesame oil and heat. Add the cornstarch mixture, then stir-fry the bell pepper 1 to 2 minutes, add mushrooms for 1 minute and then the snow peas for 1 minute. Pour in the hot broth or water and cook, covered, about 2 minutes. Spread noodles on a plate and place vegetables on top.

Serves 4

Each Serving Provides:
444 calories, 13g protein, 3g fat, 95g carbohydrate,
3mg cholesterol, 2g dietary fiber, 509mg sodium

New Mexican Vegetable Ragout

Preparation time: 30 minutes

The flavors of the Southwest come through in this vegetable mixture that is a snap to make and very filling. Serve with a salad or with corn tortillas.

4 new potatoes, diced
3 tablespoons vegetable or olive oil
1 red bell pepper, seeded and diced
1 green bell pepper, seeded and diced
3 cloves garlic, minced
2 tablespoons good-quality chili powder
2 cups corn kernels, fresh (cut from 4 ears) or frozen
1 can (28 ounces) stewed tomatoes with juice
3 cups cooked black beans or canned and drained
3 tablespoons minced fresh cilantro

Cook the potato in boiling water until just soft, about 10 minutes, then drain under cool water to stop the cooking. Heat the oil and sauté the peppers 4 minutes, add garlic and chili powder and stir to blend. Add the potato, corn, tomatoes, and black beans and simmer until the potato is tender, about 12 minutes. Stir in the cilantro and simmer another 2 minutes.

Serves 4

Each Serving Provides:
608 calories, 23g protein, 13g fat, 108g carbohydrate,
0mg cholesterol, 18g dietary fiber, 628mg sodium

Asparagus & Walnuts with Eggs

Preparation time: 20 minutes

This is a frittata, sort of an Italian answer to quiche. It's served as an entrée and can be enjoyed hot or cold.

2 slices of whole wheat bread with crusts removed
$^1/_4$ cup skim milk
10 ounces fresh asparagus, trimmed
3 eggs
3 egg whites
$1^1/_2$ ounces (about 6 tablespoons) freshly grated
    Parmesan cheese
$1^1/_2$ ounces (about 6 tablespoons) chopped walnuts
1 tablespoon chopped fresh basil
$^1/_8$ teaspoon salt
$^1/_8$ teaspoon pepper
1 to 2 teaspoons olive oil

Soak the bread in the milk for 10 minutes. Cook asparagus in boiling water for a minute or two, then rinse in cold water to stop the cooking, and drain. Cut into 2-inch pieces and set aside.

Whisk eggs and egg whites with the Parmesan and walnuts. Add the soaked bread, basil, and spices. Mix well. Heat oil in a nonstick skillet over medium heat and pour in the egg mixture, then sprinkle in the asparagus pieces. Cook until firm, 6 or 7 minutes, flip and cook until desired doneness. Slice into wedges.

Serves 4

Each Serving Provides:
256 calories, 16g protein, 17g fat, 11g carbohydrate,
168mg cholesterol, 2g dietary fiber, 427mg sodium

Roasted Pepper Potato Casserole

Preparation time: 30 minutes

This unusual combination came about by combining two foods I like best: potatoes and peppers.

2 tablespoons olive oil
2 leeks, finely chopped
12 very small new potatoes
3 carrots, sliced
5 cloves garlic, minced
2 cups vegetable broth or water
3 tablespoons chopped parsley
1 roasted red bell pepper (see page 14), chopped, or jarred
6 tablespoons vegetable oil
1 teaspoon ground coriander
$^1/_2$ teaspoon turmeric
1 cup peas, fresh or frozen

Heat olive oil in a large pot and sauté the leeks until soft, about 5 minutes. Add potatoes and carrots and cook, stirring to prevent sticking, another 7 to 8 minutes. Add garlic, broth, and parsley. Cover and simmer 10 minutes.

Combine roasted pepper, vegetable oil, coriander, and turmeric in a blender and purée to a paste. Stir into the potato mixture, along with the peas, cover, and cook another 8 to 12 minutes, until vegetables are done.

Serves 4 to 6.

Each Serving Provides:
343 calories, 5g protein, 19g fat, 40g carbohydrate,
0mg cholesterol, 4g dietary fiber, 218mg sodium

American Ghivetch

Preparation time: 25 minutes (plus 1 hour 50 minutes cooking time)

This is my version of a classic Eastern European dish filled with vegetables. It takes time to prepare but will give you 2 or 3 nights' worth of dinners. You can substitute other vegetables for the ones named here.

3/4 cup olive oil
3 cloves garlic, minced
2 teaspoons minced fresh thyme or 1 teaspoon dried
2 teaspoons minced fresh oregano or 1 teaspoon dried
1 teaspoon minced fresh basil or 1 teaspoon dried
3 tablespoons minced fresh parsley
1/8 teaspoon hot pepper sauce
1 eggplant, cubed
2 zucchinis, sliced
2 onions, halved and sliced
2 medium new potatoes, peeled and sliced
3 stalks celery, sliced
1/2 cabbage, shredded
2 cups cauliflower pieces
2 cups broccoli pieces
2 carrots, sliced
1 green bell pepper, seeded and diced
1 cup trimmed and cut green beans
2 tomatoes, peeled, seeded, and sliced

Preheat oven to 350°. Combine the olive oil, garlic, herbs, and hot pepper sauce in a bowl and set aside. In a lightly oiled pot or casserole layer vegetables, except tomatoes, and brush each layer with oil and herb mixture. Cover tightly and bake 90 minutes. Place tomatoes on top and bake another 20 minutes.

Serves 6 to 8

Each Serving Provides:
302 calories, 6g protein, 21g fat, 27g carbohydrate,
0mg cholesterol, 7g dietary fiber, 51mg sodium

Greek Potatoes & Tomatoes

Preparation time: 40 minutes

This entrée is similar to many dishes prepared daily in the villages of Greece. Good with vegetable or cucumber salad.

2 tablespoons extra-virgin olive oil
5 cloves garlic, minced
1 onion, chopped
2 cups tomato sauce
2 cups water
7 to 8 new potatoes, peeled and quartered
1/4 cup chopped fresh parsley
3/4 cup crumbled feta

Heat oil in a skillet and sauté the garlic and onion over low heat until soft, about 10 minutes. Add tomato sauce and water, bring to a boil, then add the potatoes and cook 30 minutes, until the sauce is thickened and potatoes are tender. Stir in parsley, remove from heat, and top with feta cheese.

Serves 4

Each Serving Provides:
386 calories, 10g protein, 12g fat, 63g carbohydrate, 19mg cholesterol, 7g dietary fiber, 994mg sodium

Stuffed Potatoes

Preparation time: 1 hour (plus 15 minutes baking time)

These twice-stuffed potatoes are a filling entrée, perfect with a green salad.

4 Russett potatoes, baked until soft
1 cup broccoli florets
1 cup cauliflower florets
1 teaspoon dried thyme
$^1/_3$ cup lowfat sour cream
$^1/_4$ cup lowfat mayonnaise
$^1/_3$ cup ricotta cheese
$^1/_2$ cup grated mozzarella cheese

Preheat oven to 400°. Scoop out insides of the potatoes and mix with broccoli, cauliflower and thyme. Stuff the potato skins with the mixture. Combine remaining ingredients and spoon over potatoes. Bake 12 minutes and serve.

Serves 4

Each Serving Provides:
382 calories, 14g protein, 12g fat, 58g carbohydrate, 34mg cholesterol, 5g dietary fiber, 238mg sodium

Index

Page numbers in **boldface** refer to recipes.

Conversion Chart

These are not exact equivalents: they've been slightly rounded to make measuring easier.

Liquid Measurements

American	Imperial	Metric	Australian
2 tablespoons (1 oz)	1 fl oz	30 ml	1 tablespoon
1/4 cup (2 oz)	2 fl oz	60 ml	2 tablespoons
1/3 cup (3 oz)	3 fl oz	80 ml	1/4 cup
1/2 cup (4 oz)	4 fl oz	125ml	1/3 cup
2/3 cup (5 oz)	5 fl oz	165ml	1/2 cup
3/4 cup (6 oz)	6 fl oz	185ml	2/3 cup
1 cup (8 oz)	8 fl oz	250ml	3/4 cup

Weights

US/UK	Metric
1 oz.	30 grams (g)
2 oz.	60 g
4 oz. (1/4 lb)	125 g
5 oz. (1/3 lb)	155 g
6 oz.	185 g
7 oz.	220 g
8 oz. (1/2 lb)	250 g
10 oz.	315 g
12 oz. (4/4 lb)	375 g
14 oz.	440 g
16 oz. (1 lb)	500 g
2 lbs	1 kg

Spoon Measurements

American	Metric
1/4 teaspoon	1 ml
1/2 teaspoon	2 ml
1 teaspoon	5 ml
1 tablespoon	15 ml

Oven Temperatures

Fahrenheit	Centigrade	Gas
250	120	1/2
300	150	2
325	160	3
350	180	4
375	190	5
400	200	6
450	230	8